CRITICAL ACCLAIM FOR ANNE RIVERS SIDDONS

JOHN CHANCELLOR MAKES ME CRY

"This delightful book of personal essays by an Atlanta woman who responds with humor and feeling to the life around her [reveals a] zany charm [and] sharp inner and outer perception."   —*Publishers Weekly*

"This book is a warm and well-written chronicle of a year in the life of a talented woman. I liked it, even though words fail me when it comes to the title."
—John Chancellor

"In tone, she reads like Judith Viorst without a Keds imprint on the ceiling. . . . She is unique. She's an original in that her essays combine humor, intimacy, and insight."   —Erma Bombeck

"A witty, thoughtful book in the tradition of Joan Didion. . . . It calls back a time when literature had a sense of extremes."   —Larry McMurtry

"Fresh and emotionally clean . . . Siddons displays the gift of telescoping two types of vision, that which sees the larger picture and that which dwells on the crisp perfect detail." —*Commercial Appeal* (Memphis, TN)

"[Siddons is] a gentle, warmhearted, graceful writer."
—*Dallas Morning News*

"Her eye is an impeccable camera. . . . A display of essays not only on the everyday events of life, but the unforgettable moments we'll never quite be able to capture again."   —*Buffalo News*

"Gloriously funny . . . You cannot fail to adore these stories."   —*Cosmopolitan*

Books by Anne Rivers Siddons

Low Country
Up Island
Fault Lines
Downtown
Hill Towns
Colony
Outer Banks
King's Oak
Peachtree Road
Homeplace
Fox's Earth
The House Next Door
Heartbreak Hotel
John Chancellor Makes Me Cry

John Chancellor Makes Me Cry

∞

ANNE RIVERS SIDDONS

HarperPaperbacks
A Division of HarperCollinsPublishers

HarperPaperbacks *A Division of* HarperCollins*Publishers*
          10 East 53rd Street, New York, N.Y. 10022

All or part of some of the chapters in this book were previously
published in *Atlanta Magazine, House Beautiful,* and *Georgia.*
This book was published by Doubleday & Company in 1975.
A hardcover edition was published in 1992 by
HarperCollins*Publishers*. It is hereby reprinted by
arrangement with the author.

This book is available on tape from HarperAudio, a division of
HarperCollins*Publishers.*

Cover illustration by Jeff Cornell

First HarperPaperbacks printing: October 1994

Printed in the United States of America

HarperPaperbacks, HarperSpotlight, and colophon are
trademarks of HarperCollins*Publishers*

❖ 10 9 8 7 6 5 4

To Katherine and Marvin Rivers,
my mother and father

Contents

FALL

Introduction

Since this book was first published in 1975, so much has changed in the rather small world it concerns that my first thought, when I knew it was to be re-released, was to go through it with a blue pencil and update feverishly. But when I reread it for the purpose of doing so, I found myself simply unable to cut and amend. The prospect was nastily like that of editing one's children . . . wiping out what they had been simply because of what they have become now. The grown child does not devalue the young one, and I don't feel that the 1992 perspective on this book devalues the 1975 one. On the main, I think these essays have held up pretty well, and that pleases me no end.

The world that surrounds us in this year of the Lord 1992 is a vastly different one, of course, and if the truth be told, not all that much better. The passage from Watergate to the Iran-Contra affair does not represent a great deal of progress, and the blithe little skip from supply-side economics to the S&L scandal and the insider-trading caper should, I suppose, surprise no one. We have come limping home from an unpopular war and marching home from an enormously popular one, but behind us we have still left death and destitution and loss. The poor, as it is pointed out in the New Testament, are always with us, but now they are largely homeless as well. Terrorism has become a way of life and AIDS a way of death, and the anchormen who present them all to us each evening are not, with a very few exceptions, a patch on the ones who made us weep each evening back then.

But there have been some spectacular candles lit in the darkness of this last decade of the century, and they truly light up the skies. Is it possible that that great twentieth-century bugaboo, Communism, was defanged practically overnight? Is there anyone on the planet whose heart did not lift and sing when the Wall came tumbling down? Has there ever been anything quite as gee-whiz-holy-cow-wonderful as the 1991 World Series?

Looking back, I see with surprise and a jot of chagrin that the woman who wrote these words is still, in many ways, the same woman. Shouldn't there have been some progress here? Isn't that what growing older is about . . . growing wiser? But no, eighteen years later, here is that Atlanta woman who still weeps copiously over the seven o'clock news, even if it's Peter Jennings who sets her off now, instead of Walter Cronkite. The woman who is still foolishly in love with the misfits and sociopaths of the animal kingdom, even if the original three miscreants have been gathered to the Big Catnip Patch and a new crew of wackos moved into their places. The lady who is still afraid of tornadoes and still loves reunions in Princeton and does not love New York in June. The stepmother who still dotes, if ineptly, on her four stepsons, even though they are mostly all married now and have introduced three visibly perfect grandchildren into the family stew.

And I think that is the point of this little book, and always was . . . that somehow, no matter what goes on around us during the gallop of time, we still manage to stay . . . us. I don't know about you, but to me that's a source of considerable comfort. I may not necessarily approve of the woman I find looking back over these pages, but I know her. She's the one I started out with. She can't fit into her cheerleader uniform anymore, but she certainly hasn't been sidelined yet.

And John Chancellor, bless him, still makes her cry.

Anne Rivers Siddons
January 10, 1992

John Chancellor Makes Me Cry

The Seven O'Clock Syndrome

I cry over the seven o'clock news.

At least three evenings a week, and in a prime week every evening. Sometimes it's just the familiar walnut-at-the-base-of-the-tongue, accompanied by an eye-sheening wash of tears which I can usually hide behind the *National Observer* or the round dome of the cat's back. (*He* spends the seven o'clock news crouched on my chest, tail in my face—from this angle he is a perfect series of ellipses—blinking serenely at God knows what inklings and oddments of his own.)

But at other times, the tears catch me unaware, a flood tide that rises up through my throat, reddening my eyes and corrugating my face truly hideously, spilling out in a guttering runnel of Revlon, prompting me to strangle and snort and rush into the bedroom for a Kleenex and my husband to sigh. He isn't callous, only accustomed. This briny ritual is my evensong, as the brief, neck-crippling, head-on-chest

1

nap before dinner ("I am not asleep, I am merely resting my eyes") is his.

It didn't start until a couple of years ago, this peculiar affliction of mine. Leaving the hermetically sealed dome of an Alabama college campus in the late fifties, I found the shining, murderous sixties a shattering enough experience, but it was with more or less normal bemusement and judicious, abstract outrage that I reacted. As a reporter for a city magazine during this decade, I found enough in my own back yard to mourn or decry, but somehow, it didn't unglue me. Some things came close; the fire storms of Selma and Cleveland, where my own friends in the news media stood to lose more than their cameras and tape recorders and half a nation stood to lose it all, wrung tears of fright and frustration from me. But others wept then, too. Those were the years when a whole generation of placid young sheep learned how to howl like starveling wolves. And there was the anguished jungle lying just beyond the world I knew, that bloomed, mature and perfect and terrible, when the bullet that shattered John Kennedy's head also cracked the skin of my world to reveal it. And the snowballing horror of watching them go, one by one—Medgar Evers, Martin Luther King, Bobby Kennedy. I cried then, furiously, blindly, for days—but so did everybody else. Almost.

Later in that decade, and into the next one, there were things that merited—and received—the cathartic ceremony of grief. Appalachia, Biafra, Vietnam, Bangladesh; ritual murder in California and bloodied, near-human seal pups in Alaska; the crippling of a man I feared and loathed, but whose life I affirmed, in a Maryland shopping center; earthquakes, fire, and the incredible, unspeakable image of a girl child half a world away, naked, arms outflung, running down a road in Vietnam. On fire.

Things, truly, to cry about. And sane people eating their dinners all over the world did.

This seven o'clock thing of mine is different.

It generally starts when our local news hits, at six-thirty. I've probably just come in from work and switched on the set in the den. First, the local big stuff: A member of the police aldermanic committee has been nailed for accepting a bribe from a creamy, smiling restaurateur and club owner who happens to live down the street from me. Two mayoral candidates are calling each other names. The sanitation workers' strike is waxing ripely into its second week. A black man in one of our yeastier ghettos—slated for urban renewal nine years ago—has shot his common-law wife and her three young daughters. A local supermarket survey has shown that meat prices jumped 11 percent this past week. The Falcons have lost—again. It's going to rain—again. The smirking station ombudsman, the one with the Frankenstein-like hairpiece, whose task it is to preserve, protect, and defend the small consumer by publicly shaming his corporate malefactor, silkily announces that the Ed Fleag family of Sweet Harmony Drive, this city, is indeed going to get a refund on the chemical toilet that blew up their camper on the interstate last month. The appallingly young critic-at-large, who resembles a cadet Cuban pimp, blasts a visiting symphony conductor to shards and mispronounces "Moussorgsky."

Except for the murdered family, surely not the stuff of tears. Rage, maybe, but not tears. Nevertheless, they begin to nibble at my sinuses like demented mice.

Then the national news, and out come the big guns. John Chancellor, chanting like a Druid who knows a dirty joke, is telling us about Watergate. No inherent grief there, for me, anyway; I fiercely love every new morsel and can't wait for the whole suppurating mess to be laid out cleanly, like the seed mass of a rotting pumpkin spread on newspaper, so we can throw the damned thing away. But the traitorous muscles around my mouth quiver.

Mr. Kissinger has done a good day's work on the Middle East imbroglio; gallant, cliff-faced Mrs. Meir smiles her smile of lopsided grandeur. One sinus pings shut like a butterfly valve.

An oil slick from a wounded tanker has slimed a section of coast, but area conservationists and kids, working together, have managed to capture, clean, and save most of the affected sea birds . . . close-up of saved sea bird. I whiffle, drawing an apprehensive glance from my husband, who had innocently thought tonight's news was the best we'd had in days.

David Brinkley says something so utterly sane, acid, and funny about the energy crisis that I wish I'd said it—or written it to my congressman. And a burping sob comes skittering up from behind my rib cage.

And then the news is over and the Hamm's Beer commercial comes on—the one with the shambling, trusting clown of a bear—and I am back scrabbling on my dressing table for a Kleenex.

I thought for a while that I was probably having some sort of nervous breakdown. I had always believed that to grow older was to lose the hurting edge of perception—a keen loss, a sad one, but mitigated by some measure of equanimity, a *little* wisdom, one or two scraps of tranquillity. Or, failing those, just a tougher hide and atrophied lachrymal glands. The process, I thought vaguely, was something like the change medical students undergo, which enables them to function in a world of idiot pain. But here was my hide, growing daily older and stretching daily thinner, like a squeaking balloon. Here were my tear ducts blooming wetly like ferns in El Yunque. Here I was, in the middle of my thirties (you're not getting older, you're just getting better), and on the fine edge of sitting down on the floor of the city's largest department store and wailing for somebody to come and get me because I simply couldn't *cope* anymore.

Nut City. No doubt about it.

Then one day, at the advertising agency where I write copy for resorts, real estate developments, and computer software, my friend Loraine, who has always been my grudging candidate for the best-dressed, coolest, chic-est, most unflappable and hung-together woman in the world, said, "I think I'm losing my mind. I burst into tears in the middle of *Cactus Flower* last night and had to leave the theater. And not only that, I heard on the radio, driving in this morning, that Lindbergh Drive was closed from Piedmont to Peachtree for repairs, and I started hyperventilating."

I loved her in that instant like the sister I don't have. Because it wasn't war, famine, pestilence, or death that got to sweet Loraine. It was *Cactus Flower* and street repairs. My own territorial madness.

Since the onset of my seven o'clock sniveling syndrome, I have thought a lot about why everything is getting under my skin. Loraine and I talk about it between agency crises, over agency coffee. My husband and I talk about it over sleeping cats and sodden Kleenex. Sometimes he leans to the theory, probably a reasonable one, that the Watergate malaise has crept into the fabric of the nation like a disease and corroded the connective tissue, and that we're all going to end up, in time, blubbering along with Walter Cronkite. I just got it earlier than most. At other times, he simply thinks that some small, vital element, as yet unidentified by medical science, has been left out of my body chemistry. Which makes me, I suppose, an emotional hemophiliac. Loraine alternately inclines to sunspots, positive ions, UFOs, and something in the soil or water, an opposite of the lithium in the soil of the town in Texas where everyone is gently and sweetly happy all the time. Alvin Toffler tells me I am suffering from future shock; Robert Coles and R. D. Laing have some interesting theories. Transactional analysis helps me refrain from screaming at my own nearest and dearest, at least some of the time.

But John Chancellor and Walter Cronkite won't transact back.

I think that's it. I think I've had a bait, as my grandmother used to say, of other people's problems—without a chance to talk back. They live in a walnut veneer box behind a screen in my den; they posture on a screen in my neighborhood theater; they lurk behind the dashboard of my car or inside coats of newsprint-and-ink armor. They come in and out of my life and bang the screen door, every day of my life—to anger me, touch me, amuse me. But I can't get to them—to rebut, comfort, or laugh with them. There are all these people in my den, in my head, in my life, and they are all asking for my time and my attention and my *self*, and we haven't even been introduced. Their lives are laminated away from me.

And so I run for comfort to my own life like I run to my refrigerator for Rocky Road ice cream when I can't balance my checkbook. I know what it tastes like. That's all I do know, really . . . the taste of my life. It is, God knows, a disorderly thing, arrhythmic, skittering, blatting around like an irregular pulse. But it is orderly in its ordinariness, it is reassuring in its familiarity, and it is mine. I own it. I can keep my finger on it. I can tot it up and leaf through it. Nobody can fool around with what there's been of it so far. My life is built of sequences. Hinged pieces that fit together like a vertebra—that simple, that intricate. Days. Months. Seasons. They are as comforting to tell as a rosary. They are talismen; I am a bead rattler. A kisser of elbows. A don't-stepper-on of cracks. It doesn't matter. These days, months, seasons, serve me well.

A year is a fine thing. Anybody's year. Here is one of mine. I dedicate it to everybody else who cries at the seven o'clock news.

WINTER

Do Not Go Gentle Into That Good Night

There is no other time in the world to me quite so melancholy, so *Weltschmerz*-sodden, as New Year's Eve. It is the beginning of winter, *my* winter, and I don't care what the calendar says about December 21. Fall ends at Thanksgiving in my book of days, and the period between Thanksgiving and December 31 is simply Christmas and nothing else, a period displaced from time, the Washington, D.C. of the calendar year.

Winter starts at 6 P.M. on New Year's Eve.

In my world, there has been too much holiday. I have spent too much money on Christmas presents—again. I have not gotten around to sending Christmas cards—again. I have been to—and given—too many parties; I have gained seven pounds; I am tired and cross, and there are eggplant-colored circles under my eyes. And there isn't, after all, peace on earth. There's been about one day too many of the brittle, strumpet Christmas tree and leathery, sugared dates and tarnished silver and snarls of satiny ribbons and paper weeping wetly in my back yard garbage cans. One too many late nights and one too many times in draggle-hemmed long skirts, one too many meals hastily scrambled together of leftover pâté and crackers.

The New Year's Eve Party looms like a radiant killer iceberg. My circle professes to hate New Year's Eve. Not for us the Babbitt-inspired paper hats and horns at midnight in a smoke-stunned nightclub; not for us the frantic kissing of a strange somebody's fat, rhinestoned wife or drunk husband; not for us the tearing bacchant gaiety and the hangovers and the making of asses of ourselves. We shall have, we say every year, small groups of warm, close friends over to sit before fragrant apple-log fires and stroke sleep-heavy cats and assess this dying year—taste it, savor it, give it its proper, gently melancholy rite of passage, affirm the hopeful new year.

And we do try. But by some bitter alchemy of this dying night, we invariably close our ranks to the very things we met to celebrate—reason, softness, nostalgia, sweetness, intimacy, quiet—and we overdo it. We eat too much, drink too much, laugh too loudly, kiss too fondly people we didn't arrive with, stay up much too late, totter home in the cold-bleared dawn with pounding temples and anesthetized consciences beginning to ache and clam dip on our black ties and Pucci pajamas, swearing that there's never been a better New Year's Eve.

But, in point of fact, the only really great New Year's Eve I can remember is the one when my husband and I both had flu and lay in bed, watching the ball descend from the top of the tower in Times Square, drinking hot tea laced with brandy and laughing in a soft, manic envelope of fever and close-ness and Courvoisier. But that was only one year—and we were sick.

Why, I wonder, this lemming-like seasonal lunacy? I suppose that all of us are as afraid of our coming win-ter as the Druids, whose mad midwinter ceremonials we have borrowed from. It is unlucky, atavistically Not Right, to go into that long dark without some sort of incandescent ritual to the gods of light who are leaving us for a while.

And so we once again start the new winter with slatternly, worn-out old souls. *Mea culpa.* Make that last one hemlock.

On my New Year's mornings, a mobcapped little Yankee scrub woman boots the cerise-satined jade out of my psyche and surveys the mess. Make scald-ing hot, bitter, coffee. Have a strong gulp of icy toma-to juice, to exorcise the sticky-fingered imps of last night's champagne. Out into the air, to feed the birds and get the paper. Put on the propitiatory black-eyed peas. If people are coming to watch the bowl games, there'll be hot soup or chili for them, and walloping, chewy black bread, and strong yellow cheese, maybe, but nothing sugared or spiced or glacéed or flambéed, or served with a maraschino cherry. My husband once asked me why I never served the sort of pretty, creamy, sculptured things other people have at their New Year's Day brunches. I'd never even thought about it. But I guess my subconscious ritual of clarify-ing, simplifying, atoning, begins when I wake up on New Year's Day.

By late afternoon on New Year's Day, I am ready to lunge at the poor, overdressed Christmas tree and rip its baubles off, to get out the vacuum cleaner. To walk miles in cold, bright air; eat nothing but fresh, peppery green watercress and cold spring water; wash my hair and take a bath in murderously hot water; put on soft, clean, faded-to-milk-blue Levi's; read James Thurber by myself in a stark white room.

I am ready to flex the flabby muscles of Will and Purpose and Productivity. "It's time to Get Back at It," my mother has said to me during her New Year's morning call for the past fifteen years; vaguely, but I know precisely what she means.

I need to Make a List. It is as basic a need to me, on New Year's night, as food, water, rest. And so, always, about dusk—New Year's resolutions.

For many years, in this sober twilight, my resolutions have leaned to the rearranging of my own Ten Rules for a Better Me. I will be Kinder. I will not Lie—not even to the woman who calls me at 8:30 A.M. on Saturday morning to ask if I'll collect for the Muscular Dystrophy drive. I will be a Better Citizen; I will put my muscle where my mouth is when it comes to the issues I really believe in. I will Do Something with My Life; no more *New York Times* crossword puzzles or seductive old Ngaio Marsh murder mysteries when I have some spare time. I will Set Priorities. I will determine, once and for all, what the major bones in my life are, and I will attend to them and weed out the rest. And so on. Ad nauseam.

I have been making New Year's resolutions far longer than I have been married. But since I have been, this marriage and this man have become the trellis on which the untidy, rococo tendrils of my life are pinned. I owe him, as they say in my part of the South. So here are a few things I resolve not to perpetrate upon him this year.

When he says, "Do you still have that twenty I gave you Monday morning?" I will not say, apprehensively, "Why? Are we out of money? Are we overdrawn again? God knows, you've got to tell me if we are. . . . I'll get a part-time job as a saleslady." My husband gets very insecure when I immediately assume the worst about money—a thing I do at least once a day. He feels that his role as keeper of the family exchequer (it has nothing to do with his being a chauvinist pig; we both believe in the women's movement; I simply cannot add) is being impugned. He is forced to answer heartily, "Of course we're not overdrawn. I merely wanted to know if you needed any more money. Here's a ten to get you through the week." If, in fact, we are overdrawn, I have cut off any possibility of our discussing it like two adults, he has lost the twenty he needed to cover the overdraft and another ten to boot, and the drugstore will righteously refuse to cash any more checks.

I will not comment that all his ex-girlfriends seem to be named Muffie or Fluffie or Buffie or Scruffie and from all reports have mentalities to match. Especially if I have never met them. Making waves where none exist is insanity. Besides, I was forced to retract this statement when I met an ex at his class reunion last summer and she turned out to be a cool, willowy, blond systems analyst for IBM with a tennis-playing investment banker husband, three beautiful and exemplary children, and a Geoffrey Beene suit. Wives who bad-mouth their husband's former flames are invariably compelled to make graceless and flat-footed retractions and end up feeling like whinnying shrews. Especially when he says, "Well, I married you, didn't I?" and you wonder if he wonders why he did.

I will not cavil, quarrel, fidget, or sigh loudly and frequently when he turns on the football game on Saturday and Sunday afternoon. Monday night, maybe, but not on Saturday and Sunday. I will not say pointedly to anyone in the room, "If you have anything to say to him, say it now, because he won't hear you again until after the Super Bowl." I will not refer to *Sports Illustrated* as an adult comic book. I will not suggest acidly that perhaps he would like my new at-home thing better if I sewed Mercury Morris's number on it, or invite my college roommates over for Bloody Marys when the Rams are playing the Falcons, or remark brightly that all men put themselves to sleep at night imagining they are intercepting Daryl Lamonica's long bomb for a fifty-yard touchdown in the last seconds of the game. I will remember, when tempted to waffle-mouth him on a Sunday afternoon, the elaborate glee I evinced at all things athletic before we were married, and the esoteric sports terms I memorized to toss into the conversation for purposes of further misrepresentation.

I will not scatter wistful remarks about When I Was Single. I will not, when passing the most over-priced, overcrowded, and pretentiously dull restaurant in town, murmur, "I wonder how the food is now. I used to go there a lot. . . . " I will not smile enigmatically when he asks, "Where did you get that bracelet?" I will not laugh merrily to old friends about "that crazy, marvelous weekend in Nassau," or chortle, "Remember the champagne party and what happened to the shower curtain?" and then say, "Oh, honey, you wouldn't be interested; you don't know any of those people." I will bear in mind that he knew me when I was single, too, and will recall, with a clarity I have conveniently misplaced, that I frequently bought (pre-ecology) alligator shoes and had to live on peanut butter the rest of the month, that my mother gave me the bracelet, and that the parade of men through my apartment was more often than not my roommates' Gentlemen Callers, who were, moreover, as broke as we were most of the time.

I will not make snide remarks about his age. I will not drum my fingers and smile thinly when he digs out his old Glenn Miller records, or snort when he sings "He Wore a Pair of Silver Wings" in the shower. I will make no more quaint observations about mating ostriches when he demonstrates his prize-winning jitterbug. I will not giggle at his Ruptured Duck or his Fifty-Mission Crush or remind him of his black-and-yellow plaid zoot suit, and "That must have been before my time" will never again cross my lips. I will try to recall, though he would never remind me, that I let him think I was considerably younger than I was until the implacable lady at the marriage license bureau forced the truth out of me—and made me repeat it twice because I mumbled.

I will not tell amusing husband stories to all and sundry. The fact that the bookcase he built fell three times, once on our cleaning lady, was the fault of ill-made molly screws or something and was funny to no one, least of all the cleaning lady. The letter from the pompous, pimply young assistant manager at the bank, written in response to a visit my husband made in my behalf to close out my maiden-name checking account, that began, "Dear Mrs. Siddons: Your father was in yesterday and asked us . . ." was a general indictment of all self-important, downy-faced young asses and was no reflection on my husband's appearance. In his tweed hat, he looks like a *Gentlemen's Quarterly* ad. The letter was certainly not funny enough to send to his mother. The fact that he once dropped a paper bag full of water on Harold Stassen from the bell tower of his university is hardly the stuff of good cocktail conversation, and neither is the usual assortment of groggy morning mix-ups with the spray dry cleaner and the Right Guard. And anyone could manage to install a swinging cat door into the top of a door, instead of the bottom, if he had it laid across two sawhorses, left the room, and came back in by a different door. He has never once told, and is far too decent to tell, a roomful of grinning people that I went to work minus my skirt one harried winter morning, or sprained my toe kicking a footstool in a fit of peevishness over a burned-out light bulb.

I will not tell anyone else the nickname he had as a baby.

I will not get up at dawn to get the Sunday crossword puzzle first.

I will not put Kleenex into the toilet, I will remember to disengage the emergency brake, and I will never, never say again to the man who backs into me in the supermarket parking lot, "That's perfectly all right. I'm sure it was my fault."

And I probably won't ever make any more New Year's resolutions. At least, not in print.

Ice

❧

On January 7 last year, the Great Ice came to Atlanta.

It was Sunday afternoon, never a good time for me, especially in winter. Old sorrows visit me then, and shabby old guilts, and a restlessness born of scattered Sunday papers, cold coffee, overheated dens, unmade beds, too long in the house, and the sure and certain knowledge of a weekend frittered away and Monday morning looming. I always think of Emily Dickinson's "There's a certain slant of light, on winter afternoons, that oppresses, like the weight of cathedral tunes." There was a lady who surely knew about Sunday afternoons.

I know that Sunday afternoon can be fought, with long walks, cooking something French, or just getting out of the house, but the effort even to dress is enervating. Nevertheless, if my husband and I are both exceedingly Sunday-stunned and in imminent danger of having a fight out of sheer boredom, I will consent to go, gracelessly, to a movie. And that's where we were when the Ice came.

Coming out of the theater as blindly as coming up from under water, we heard the hiss first. Georgia ice, when it is in earnest, comes down, not with a crystal tinkle, but an eerie, ominous hiss. Cars were already sheeted with pocked, opaque ice. Pellets like rock salt caromed off an inch or more slush on the parking lot. The sky was stretched tight and soiled white and spilling ice out of its gut, steadily. We knew we were in for it.

We have one or more ice storms each winter, and they are not so welcome here as the fickle, pretty snows. Traffic is lethal on ice. Pine branches go down; power lines sag under the weight and sometimes snap, darkening parts of the city for hours. Bones are broken and camellias are blasted black, and die.

But the next morning, according to the script, the sun is out, and all the city is a Tiffany window, and people who can't get to work or school put on old clothes and slither out, laughing and skidding, to admire their diamond neighborhoods. By noon, streets have gone to wet black again, and cautious motorists can range farther afield, to see what chandeliers the ice has hung on other streets. Weather is usually the stuff of holidays in Atlanta, heady and giddy-making.

This was different. We were silent on the treacherous drive home. Something enormous and impersonal crouched in the sky, something malignant and very old. Ice stung down and mounted up, and you knew no sun-jeweled Winter Carnival was going to be held the next day. At the 7-Elevens and Pot o' Golds along the way, cars were clustered, and people were dumping loads of firewood and charcoal into their trunks.

It doesn't take the age-old, neck-prickling smell of siege long to permeate a city.

We stopped at the unabashedly overpriced and resourceful convenience emporium on the corner of Peachtree Road and our street. "Firewood," I said mindlessly to Heyward. "And soup. And milk. And, oh, yes—a loaf of bread." I wonder why it is that you automatically think of bread when weather threatens. We hardly ever eat it.

We got the last armload of wood—miserable, green, soaked, whitened with wet lichens. Already someone had marked through the original price with a grease pencil and upped it, an omen worse than the sibilant sky.

That night, cooking dinner with an ear cocked to the weather bulletins on the TV, I was nervous and unsettled. I thought of the dreadful morning, years ago, when Russian ships steamed toward the American barricade off the Cuban coast, and we all waited silently to see if we were going to be at war, dead, or merely frightened witless. It was almost the same feeling. Outside the kitchen, the ice shawled down. I turned the heat up. Finally, prowling and unhappy, we went to bed.

About 2 A.M., the first transformer blew. It made a hollow, deadened boom. Another followed, and another. We came awake with scalps crawling, scrambling to windows to pull back the drapes. The great, unknown noise in the night that you have feared since you were very young is even more terrible when it finally comes.

In the dark, great unearthly green and blue flowers

bloomed, sparks arced and showered, the warlike booms ran down our street like spilled mercury from a broken thermometer. You could hear the thunder, muted, on other streets. The house was cold and dead, electricity gone. Cats were flattened under the bed, a moratorium tacitly declared in their war. We could hear shrieking, rending, unending splits, followed by titan crashes—no branches, those. Our street is carved through dense, two-hundred-foot hardwoods. Trees were coming down.

The rest of that night we huddled under all the blankets in the house, wearing tennis socks and sweaters, listening to the ice beast raging outside, straining particularly for the death shrieks of the colossal oaks and hickories that lean close over our house.

In the morning, there was ruin.

Our street, cloistered away in an old neighborhood and lined with two-story white wood or stone dowager houses, looked shabby, desolated, defeated, bombed. Live wires whipped and whispered, snakelike, on lawns and in the street. Telephone poles leaned drunkenly, caught in the webbing of slack wires, or lay splintered across Vermont Road. But it was the great trees, the pride of us all, that broke hearts—giants were down, splintered twenty feet up, or pulled from the earth like uprooted dandelions, leaving meteorlike craters, their root systems towering twice the height of a man's head. One monster white oak had gone through a roof across the street. We felt sickened and humbled, as if a demented war had missed its appointment someplace else, broken over Atlanta, and left as suddenly as it had come. We were lucky at our house; our trees leaned, yawed—but held.

There was no way to tell the extent of the damage. Power was gone; transistor radios were the only link with the city, with the world. We had none. But the house was cold, and it was dark, and the wet wood we had bought the day before refused to burn in our fireplace.

Outside, oddly, the streets were clear of ice. But the mercury stayed implacably at thirty degrees, and the skies still hung tumescent and ice-promising. Wanting to get warm, to huddle with my fellow creatures, to share and be comforted, I took an icy sponge bath in my shadowy bathroom, dressed, and crept carefully to work, skirting along the few streets that were relatively clear of trees and power lines. The damage was worse than we could have dreamed; along Peachtree Road in to downtown, where my agency is, there were no neon signs, no traffic lights, no signs of light or warmth in darkened stores and office buildings. The car radio said that three fourths of the city was stricken dark and that the Georgia Power Company had sent out emergency calls to units in ten states for help. The mayor had declared a state of extreme emergency. There were repeated urgings for the few neighborhoods with electricity to take in as many stricken families as possible for the duration—and it looked like a long duration. The weather bureau reported that temperatures would stay below freezing for several days, that high winds were threatening the ice-brittled trees that still stood, and that more ice was a distinct possibility. Atlanta was as helpless as a turtle on its back, and people who lived on the creamy, affluent streets where warmth and light had always been an unquestioned, basic fact of life shivered helplessly for the first time in their lives. Only in the ghettos, used to cold, were there such things as gasoline and kerosene heaters. And they have always been the winter death-dealers, as well as comforters.

By noon that day, most large commercial buildings in the city's heart had their power back, and there was not a motel or hotel room to be had in the city. Stores operating by candlelight were out of gasoline lanterns, firewood, candles, and sterno by dusk. In a few shameful instances, prices for necessities soared out of sight. Happily, even in the crisis, those stores were largely boycotted.

At my agency, and in offices all over the city, there was the sort of reckless gaiety that must have electrified London during the blitz. "My hardships are worse than your hardships" became the order of the day. That first day, no one at my office had power at home, and people with gas kitchen stoves and working fireplaces, who could at least eat hot food and sleep warmly on living room and den floors, were almost apologetic about it, almost ostracized by the rest of us. We were reluctant, that evening, to leave the warmth and light of the building, and gallons of hot coffee were drunk. No work was done.

On that second evening, those of us with inoperable fireplaces and no gas stoves gave up the ghost. I am, I find, not emotionally equipped to be both cold and dirty. Cravenly, we loaded the car with clothes, a few things from the freezer that we thought might be saved, and spitting, wailing cats; locked the house and disconnected the main power switch (an act that reminded me, in its futility, of Scarlett O'Hara locking the front door of Miss Pittypat's house in the face of the advancing Yankee army); and crept off to my

parents' house in Fairburn, twenty miles away. Fairburn, by some caprice of the storm, lost no lights and
heat. There wasn't enough room for us all, and the
rapidly escalating war between my tomcats and my
parents' manic Siamese made the nights hideous with
thumping skirmishes and the bone-marrow-chilling
Siamese War Cry—but we were warm and clean and
well fed. We were luckier than most.

My husband and I drove into Atlanta each morning that week to our offices. And each day, we waited
for the lights to come on again in the city. They
didn't—and each day's weather forecast was more
ominous than the last. Power crews from as far away
as Kentucky and Arkansas were in the city now, a
small army of cold, exhausted men, working in shifts
around the clock. Residents who had the means to
make it kept pots of hot coffee coming to them
through the day. People crowded to restaurants and
lingered as long as decency allowed, some with sleeping children in booths alongside them, or sat through
movies twice and three times.

Slowly, one by one, neighborhoods began to
bloom again. On the third day, two people at my
agency had power. On the fourth, about half did. Day
five saw almost everyone warm and well fed again.
On day six, my boss and I were the lone bereft ones.
We felt persecuted, cut out of the herd, and took each
newly warmed and lit home as personal affronts.
Friends' stories of meals cooked over open fireplaces,
sleep snatched in front of fires in blankets and sleeping bags, Monopoly games and ghost stories by fire
and candlelight, were gay and nostalgic in retrospect—
but not to the people in my neighborhood. We
learned later that our section of North Atlanta had

been hardest hit, being first in the path of the storm as it came in from Chattanooga. We're almost proud of that now, as though our mettle had been the most severely tested, and we passed.

But on that sixth day, there wasn't one of us who wouldn't have sold our cringing souls for a hot bath, a warm bed, and a working television set.

Late in the afternoon of Friday, January 12—six days into the siege—there was an emergency weather bulletin. More ice by evening, it said, and subfreezing temperatures and high winds. People who had just gotten their power back were frantic. People who had none yet were desperate. I burst into tears.

But the ice demons were tired of us, I suppose, because the new ice never came. In the morning, a sheepish, repentant sun came sidling out. Our nice next-door neighbors on Vermont Road, who'd stuck it out while we had fled, called us in Fairburn: The lights were on. Back into the car, with cabin-fever-maddened cats and mounds of dirty clothes and food pressed on us by my poor, harried mother. Both parents bravely waved us off, saying that it hadn't been a bad week at all; it was nice to be together as a family again, "anytime you need us, of course, we're here." But I'm sure they had a genteel, private Saturnalia as we rolled, Okie-like, out of their driveway.

After a day or two of tossing rancid food out of the refrigerator and freezer and scrubbing them with soda, after piling in comforting stocks of groceries and scrubbing floors, after chain-sawing and stacking what fallen limbs we could physically handle, we were pretty much back to normal. Damage throughout the city, we heard, ran into the millions, mostly from trees and roofs and automobiles, and those were only first estimates. But the lights were on in Atlanta again. A week or two later, the Reign of Terror had receded into the stuff of cocktail conversation, as Tarawa and the Ardennes seem to have done after World War II. That, I suppose, is one way you know when a war is truly over.

We aren't really the same, though; at least I'm not. Something in me that was a pigtailed child skipping through a flower bed and never noticing the damage is older, now, and frailer. There has been a loss of innocence of a kind, and the birth of a sort of sneaking, hand-wringing fear of which I am not proud. I was never apprehensive about weather before; we do not live in real storm country. And what ills and woes that have directly touched my fortunate life up to now have been, in part, of my own making, or at least comprehensible. Nothing casually, dreadfully impersonal has devastated me or mine so far.

But now, that peculiar, stinging wet edge to a gray winter day frightens me, seriously and badly. Prowling winds make me uneasy. I look far more into the sky, at the clouds. It was there all along, I think, some atavistic old weather-fear, but in my case, buried under many years of warmth, privilege, convenience, control, the city.

That old, old weather wisdom, that certainty of vulnerability to impersonal chaos, is what has separated my generation from the ones who came before me. They knew it as intimately as their own skins, as soon as they were old enough to reason; in knowing it, a compensating toughness and resiliency were born early in them. I've always fancied that, having a fairly well-developed spirit of adventure and a taste for new experiences, I would have made a splendid frontier woman, a fine pioneer. I found, one week in January, that I wouldn't have made it past the Mississippi River without shrieking for them to circle the wagons.

Willa Cather wouldn't have wasted a squiggle of ink on the likes of me. But I read her, now, with new respect.

Whee! The Jury!

❦

The city had scarcely finished picking up the debris from the Great Ice Capade when two things happened, one to me and one to the city. I received my first summons for jury duty. And, like a child sticking its tongue out after setting fire to the garage, winter dealt us a small snow.

"By virtue of the precept directed to me, you are hereby commanded to appear before the Presiding Judge of the Superior Court of Fulton County, Courtroom 404 in the Court House in the City of Atlanta, to be sworn in as a *Petit Juror*," said the blue wisp of officialese in the mailbox. "Hoooo, boy, now you're really going to get the old slice of life," said my husband, an ardent judiciphile who has never served on a jury. "It's a civic duty we are happy to have you perform," said my employers. "You'd better leave an hour early if you want a parking place," said my practical lawyer father, who is in and out of the courthouse several times a week. "Do make friends with

29

some nice lady," said my gentle mother, who is still reverberating from jury duty on a rape case several years back.

So, on an icy Monday morning, streets still glazed with the remnants of the after-all trivial snow and cars careening tipsily off curbs and other cars, I set out at 8 A.M. to discharge my civic duty, and got to the courthouse at 9:10. The Fulton County Courthouse has, among its many brass-and-marble attributes, the most relaxed elevators in town. It was 9:20 when I sidled into Courtroom 404, fully expecting a blue-jawed bailiff to challenge me to show cause why I was twenty minutes late delivering myself to the hands of the court as an instrument of public justice. Instead, I found a vast, paneled room full of grave-faced, overcoated citizens, wet collars and still-slushy boots testifying to the fact that they, too, had just puffed in. Justice may not, as it claims, wait on any man (or is that time?) but it's putty in the hands of an inch-deep Atlanta snowfall.

Jury duty in the Superior Court of Fulton County generally involves a week of one's time. It is a long week. Few jurors serve on more than one case, and many never serve at all. After the first morning, when the three hundred or so people assembled in the large courtroom were assigned to consecutively numbered panels of twelve, everyone retired to the jury room, a large, stunningly bland room we came to call the Green Room, in honor of the dreary cubicles where performers waiting their turn on TV variety and panel shows are purported to sweat out their pre-Carson purgatories. In this Green Room, there are rows of chrome and Naugahyde chairs, a few round tables with more chairs drawn up to them, mulish machines to dispense coffee, soft drinks, candy, and cigarettes. (The one dime out of the many I trustingly inserted into them that ever produced any results at all caused the coffee machine to keep the cup and pour my coffee down its gurgling drain.) A loud-speaker occasionally requested nasally that panels three, nine, and eleven report to Judge So-and-So's courtroom at once, and three bodies of twelve good men and true would rise and troop out, their faces immobile with the sober resolve of moral responsibility. The rest of us, full, we were sure, of untapped resources of whatever it is that produces rare and exceptional jurors, looked after them with resentment, squirming for the chance to show our own stuff. Soon the rejected jurors—and sometimes four or five panels are sifted through before an acceptable panel of twelve is obtained—began to trickle back. They looked, to a man, crestfallen and apologetic, as if their rejection might have been the result of a credit check or denture breath. The rest of us, smug and vindicated, smiled warmly upon them. It wasn't long before the tight regiments began to break into small groups and cliques. "What do *you* do?" and "Have you seen *Last Tango in Paris* yet?" were exchanged. We became, if not a family, at least voyagers on the same ship for a week.

A roomful of prospective jurors waiting to be impaneled is, to my mind, the truest cross section of humanity any of us is likely to encounter. There is no stratification as to occupation, income, neighborhood, race, sex, color, creed, or any of the anxious pecking orders we impose upon ourselves to keep our worlds warm and neat. As the lady who sat next to me in the long Naugahyde line—a nice lady who had brought along a paperback *Goren on Bridge*, just the person my mother meant me to make friends with— put it, "It takes all kinds." It certainly does. And somehow, the task we were there to discharge, the somber but titillating sense of individual destinies waiting to be put into our hands, brought out the innermost, quivering, unvarnished essences of us. Good, bad, silly, sober, prejudiced, compassionate, pretentious, forthright . . . our "company" veneers gave way the first morning.

There was an elderly lady, round and smooth as a chinaberry, talcum-scented and elastic-stockinged, who joined me for lunch in the courthouse cafeteria the second noon. I had seen her, the center of a clump of near-identical ladies at one of the round tables, eating an endless procession of chocolate-covered raisins and intoning to each other in a sort of ageless, unceasing Greek chorus about various gyne-cological outrages that had been perpetrated upon their friends, relatives, and acquaintances. When the litany dropped below a certain level of sound, I assumed they had gotten around to their own private Bergen-Belsens. She was, she said to me over her macaroni and cheese, a maiden lady and grateful to be one. Her prime ambition was to serve as a juror on a rape case, preferably one involving a minor. "But they won't call me," she assured me. "No defense attorney would have me on his jury for love or money. They can tell when they interview you whether you're going to let the scum off or not. They'll take a man any day; men'll always sympathize with a rapist secretly. I say hanging's too good for 'em." (When I broke in to inform her that the Supreme Court had outlawed the death penalty and

that Georgia had never hung anybody anyway, preferring the dubious merits of the electric chair, I don't
think she heard me.) "Nope, they'll never call me,"
she went on. "No lawyer in the world can change my
mind about one of those animals, and they'd see it
right off." I don't know if any rape cases were tried
that week, but I do know that the lady was finally
impaneled on an insurance claim case that lasted the
rest of the week and ran over into the next. She must
have been terribly disappointed.

On the third morning, after all the copies of the
National Geographic and *Commercial Fertilizer
World* had been read and people were getting chattier
and more restive, a square, gray-haired, gray-eyed,
gray-suited gentleman started a conversation with
me. He was one of the loftier executives in a national
firm headquartered in Atlanta, he confided; he
belonged to three clubs, five civic organizations, had
a son at Harvard and another pulling down a very
creditable salary on the West Coast, and raised prize
dahlias. "It's a pity our womenfolks have to go
through this," he murmured solicitously. "Are you
getting along all right?" I wondered what Gloria
Steinem would have said to him, but, after all, only
told him that I was fine, thank you, I hadn't gone
through anything at all yet, and it didn't look like I
ever would. But I was looking forward to serving on a
jury. He was appalled. He had heard of a case tried
last week, one whose jury had been made up largely
of women. It was another rape case. (Rape seems to
have great popular appeal among jurors.) The victim
was a young Korean girl, an exchange student at an
Atlanta university, and he recounted the case to me in
shatteringly graphic detail, peering moistly into my

face while he talked, presumably to see if I was going to get the vapors. The women on that jury, he said, had been victimized by the court. No woman ought to have to listen to that. Wondering why, then, he had told me about it, I asked, "What about the girl it happened to? Do you think she particularly enjoyed having to talk about it again?" That, he thought, was a little different. Orientals were used to that sort of thing.

There were brighter spots by far than that man. There was a young girl, everyone's pet, a radiant child with two young children and a husband who was a fireman, whose incandescent face and sweet chatter were pure delight. Her sheer joy in her babies and her house, her delight in all of us, and the awesome excitement of maybe being on a jury ("Imagine me on a jury!") was clean and contagious and very, very happy. She was fiercely determined to be absolutely impartial even if she didn't like the defendant very much ("And I know it's sort of hard to like people who've done some of the things they tell you about, but what if it was me or Andy up there?"). She was rejected for two panels and was convinced it was because she stuttered when they asked her to state her name and address. It was too bad. She would have made a fine juror.

Toward the end of the week, I was accepted for duty on a shoplifting case and met a fellow juror, a lady I will remember the rest of my days, though I have already forgotten her name. The merchandise in question—a bright red coat and dress ensemble—had been taken from a department store in a fashionable northside shopping center. The defendant was a black man, and the lady's mind was made up before she set foot in the jury room. "Of course, he's guilty," she told us upon entering the little room behind the courtroom. "They like red. Did you ever notice that? Anything bright'll get their eye, but red especially." The case was not an open-and-shut one; eventually, we found the man guilty, though many of us had reservations throughout the proceedings, and a long, heated debate about "reasonable doubt" ensued at one point. But that lady never entertained a doubt, reasonable or otherwise, about the man's guilt. And she told us so, loudly and often. Our exasperated foreman, a soft-spoken and eminently reasonable red-headed Irishman, asked her early in the day to keep her mind open; he told her that we were dealing with a felony and the sentence that could result from a felony was no small thing to toss off without thought. "Oh," said the lady, "a felony. I thought it was a crime."

She was cordially disliked by the rest of us, and the foreman finally got in a workmanlike bit of retribution that warmed our hearts. "Now," he said to her as we waited to return to the courtroom and present our finding to the judge, "don't worry about the post-trial interview with the defendant. You won't be alone with him more than two minutes, and all you'll have to do is tell him very honestly why you had to find him guilty. It's not bad, and we all have to do it. It's his right. And there'll be an armed guard right outside the door."

As we trooped back into the courtroom, she hung back, and I heard her ask the bailiff if the judge would excuse her from the post-trial interview. She had had a heart condition since she was a girl, she said, and her doctor had been opposed to her serving

on a jury in the first place, but she had never been
one to shirk her duty. The interview, however, just
might be too much for her poor, tired heart. . . .

I don't know what he told her, and I didn't see her
again after we were dismissed, but I hope it embarrassed her.

Flu

∞

Once a winter, usually in the mottled, liver-colored hiatus between the holidays and the first lemon-frost flush of forsythia, flu gets into my house. I don't mean the goose-honking colds brought on by slogging senselessly from my office to the hairdresser's in cobwebby suede sandals, or the ringing, pounding sinus attacks caused by nothing at all. This is the real thing, fever-floating, magnificently aching, the kind of malaise that leaves your legs rubbery and tentative for weeks and is impervious to vitamin C, aspirin, and the anonymous tablets my doctor sends from the drugstore whose names end in -in.

My husband gets it first. "My throat feels funny," he says sadly one evening, and I run for the Coricidin; hopelessly, because my head-it-off measures have never headed off any affliction he has ever had. He gets sick very seldom, but when he does, it is baroque

beyond belief and worthy of a chapter in Thomas
Mann's *The Magic Mountain.*

This year, it began, traditionally, with a scratchy
throat around 10 P.M. Dosed and stunned with whatever we had left over from last year's siege, he went
to bed. I heard the dreaded, dry, tight coughing start
around midnight, and the wumping, murmuring
rolling that means fever and aching about four
o'clock. At five he sat bolt upright, announced that
his left knee hurt like hell, and slumped back into a
heavy, clammy sleep. Oh, God, I thought tiredly,
knowing we had precisely two weeks—not a day
more or less—of flu to get through. One week for
him, one for me. It was Monday morning. I wanted to
cry.

At six he got up to stagger into the bathroom and
bellowed, "Goddammit! The cat threw up and I
stepped in it!" Raising up to look, I saw indeed that
the cat had, and indeed he had. I did cry, a few weak,
tired, self-pitying tears. And then I got up and
cleaned up the cat vomit, coaxed three aspirins and a
cup of hot tea down the victim, flung the cat out of
the room, and got ready to go to work.

The first day of husband-flu is a terrible thing.
You know that the juices, the aspirin, the nasal
sprays, the hot broths are not going to help at all, but
you keep them coming anyway, in the witless hope
that they'll make the duration of "this thing that's
going around" shorter. (Doctors never call it flu,
perhaps on the theory that one's knowing that it's
going around is vaguely comforting to victim and
family.) *This* first morning, however, was worse than
my wildest nightmares. On Mondays, my agency has
a 9 A.M. meeting to review the state of our corporate

world; no one cares if you're a bit late on other days, but this meeting, come earthquake or market crash, is not to be missed. Between dosing man and beast and trying not to make any noise in the bedroom, I was already running late. It was pouring rain outside, a circumstance that transforms Atlanta's already hideous Monday morning traffic into a Gothic horror. The men who had *not* come to fix the leak in the den roof for three weeks came, stood puddling in the kitchen, explaining reasonably why they couldn't be expected to fix a leak in a downpour, and departed. My umbrella having been lent to the maid the week before, I waded out to the car and, cursing and dripping, nosed it into the metallic lava of traffic already clogging Peachtree Road. I had gotten perhaps a half block before the trunk lid rose up like a surfacing Loch Ness monster and flapped gently and rhythmically, blocking whatever teeming vision I had in my rearview mirror. (You have to slam it hard, and someone hadn't.) Getting out into the rain to slam it, and effectively blocking the middle lane of traffic, I heard the first horn start. By the time I'd gotten back in business, my lane was congealed for a mile back and blaring like the brass section of every band in Macy's Thanksgiving Parade. I gave one and all an obscene gesture, which served to heighten the cacophony precisely as though some cosmic orchestra conductor had brought in the bassoons. I was, of course, late to the meeting.

Day two is a suspended sort of stage in our flu. Nothing happens. By this time, frightened by all the tales of Spanish Influenza in 1918 I ever heard and vaguely angry at my husband (an inexplicable, tense state I get into every time he gets sick), I have called our doctor and gotten a prescription. But it hasn't had time to work yet. The victim sleeps. And sleeps. I call him from work to wake him for his pill; his voice sounds far away and feeble, nastily evocative of the Voice from the Grave. In the evening, he sips consommé madrilene and sleeps. I sip nervous vodka and orange juice, the vodka to quell the "He's going to die of complications" certainty and the orange juice to combat his microbes.

For they are all over the house now, like soldier ants. In the snowdrifts of crumpled tissues. In the four thousand juice glasses I have hauled to the dishwasher. In the tangled bedclothes, the cats' fur, on the bathroom mirror, on his aged, disreputable Brooks Brothers pajamas. These relics must be of immeasurable comfort to him; I see them only when he is ill. He eschews pajamas when he is well.

Day three, and he has not died during the long night. Indeed, when he wakes, he is cooled and chastened and sees me, I think, for the first time since the flu hit. This is my morning to start my campaign to get bedclothes and pajamas changed and him bathed and shaved. "You have no idea how much better you'll feel," I plead, but it is I who'll feel better. His haunted, beard-rimmed, blear-eyed countenance makes me feel guilty, as though I had been neglecting a survivor of Dachau. But a tottering trip to the bathroom delays the project. He is dizzy. "Tonight," he croaks. "And would you bring some magazines home?"

So I arrive home bearing magazines and navel oranges, and walk into the absolute nadir of influenza. The bedroom has that peculiar sweet, damp, musty sick smell. Gray, limp sheets are pulled loose from the bottom of the bed and swaddle him like a six-foot Baby Jesus. Newspapers and Kleenex litter every flat surface, sticky medicine spoons are glued to the mahogany night table, the furnace is roaring at 85 degrees, cream of asparagus soup with putty skin has congealed in saucepans in the kitchen. Victim is querulous, testy, depressed, bored, and still sick. This is my most unfavorite day. We have a weak, half-hearted quarrel and go to bed.

Day four. *Much* better. He showers, shaves, suffers clean sheets and fresh air, eats a hot breakfast, and thinks he'll go in to work for a little while in the afternoon. "Don't be an idiot," I snarl. "You'll have a relapse." He goes in to work. He has a relapse.

Day five and he is weak but lucid, consents to stay home but prowls unhappily. This is the day he will decide to start papering the bathroom, or hang his hideous pictures of Nassau Hall, painted on glass, in the living room—a running intramural skirmish that flares into open hostility once or twice a year. I am by now feeling frumpy, unattractive, cream-soup-clotted, bored with the ministering-angel bit, and ready to scream at the television set.

Next day, he goes in to work for half a Saturday, to catch up, and is tired, but that's all. And the next, Sunday, he's reborn and refreshed and in love with sweet life and avid to get back in touch with the good earth and the world of well people. We see a movie and stop for pizza on the way home. Somehow, I hate the anchovies, and the wine pools thickly just below my tongue. I don't like any of the people there, either; they look mean and squinty, and their gabble hurts my head.

"I have a sore throat," I say sadly, getting ready for

bed. "Oh, God," he says. Feeling the queer, sick-behind-my-eyes sensation start, I get into bed. I know what it means, of course, and am fairly frantic, but I feel cravenly vindicated, too.

His turn.

The Animal Farm and the
Time of the Possum

"What is it about you," my husband asked one morning recently in the tone he uses when he really doesn't expect an answer, "that attracts rare, exotic, or just plain screwy animals?" He was watching our friendly Orkin man, who drops in one Saturday morning a month to spray our environs with the malodorous alchemy he carries in his shoulder tank, as he examined with a certain professional reverence what seemed to me to be a pretty tough customer of a common cockroach. "This," said our intrepid exterminator, "is absolutely the first German cockroach I've seen in fifteen years." It was obvious that we had made his day, and I wondered if he'd tell his peers at coffee break about the house out on Vermont Road that had, by God, a German cockroach in the kitchen.

Housewife, U.N. delegate, or daughter of joy, there isn't a woman alive, I am sure, who doesn't view the intrusion of cockroaches as tangible, scurrying evidence of personal sloth, if not downright cosmic inferiority. But to harbor the first German cockroach to defile Fulton County in fifteen years makes you feel both slatternly and unjustly singled out. So my husband's pointedly theatrical observation, staged expressly for the benefit of the Orkin man in order to absolve himself from any blame in the German Cockroach Caper, rankled triplefold. "That's not fair," I bristled, stung at being exposed to the Orkin man's scorn. "You make me sound like some kind of Pied Piper for four-legged nuts."

"Exactly," he rejoined. "You've had stray animals carousing around you ever since I've known you, and not one of them has been normal. Some of them aren't even sane."

"Found a spotted domino moth on the living room windowsill last month," put in the Orkin man, obviously settling in for a seminar on Lepidoptera. "Now them fellers are *really* hard to come by. Last one I found was in . . ."

But I had gone into the bedroom and shut the door.

My husband is right, though. I love animals. I cannot watch the Walt Disney specials about cunning coyotes or valiant kangaroo rats, even though I know Everything Will Come Right in the End. Mashed squirrels wring an involuntary "It's all right now, baby," from me on my way to work. Dead dogs and cats destroy my day. The appearance of a dog in a television drama leads me to conclude instantly that he's being set up for maiming or death at the hands of the villains, else he wouldn't be there at all, and so I leave the room. When the Humane Society set up an adoption branch on my route to work down Peachtree Road, I simply had to find another route. The sight of those wire cages through the plate-glass windows evoked such a blur of tears that I was a menace on the road. The most rudimentary trick laboriously mastered by the most cretinous dog in Christendom is a wonderment to me. Once, I almost bought a coatimundi out of a shopping-center pet shop window because, with his head on his crossed paws and his eyes cast up at the world, he simply broke my heart. That plan, fortunately, was thwarted.

And it's true, we do seem to get an uncommon number of strays around our house, of all species, all of whom I assiduously feed, water, and croon over. It's equally true that most of them are belligerent, manic, or out-and-out weirdos.

The Number One Cat, Peter Quint, is a case in point. He wasn't a stray. He was a gift, from the Machiavellian editor of the magazine I worked for at the time, who shamelessly took advantage of my propensity for losers and brought him to our doorstep, trembling and meowing and sodden, in a violent rainstorm one night. But he is unmistakably a stray in all but the accident of his birth. And he is a working weirdo.

In the early days of his tenure with us, he behaved much as homesick kittens are supposed to, howling dismally during the nights from atop the refrigerator and shooting sideways in an ungainly sort of crablike shuffle. He was a lank, spidery, laconic sort of kitten who never turned a whisker at his grandiose name, borrowed from the terrible, red-haired ghost in *The Turn of the Screw*, and would answer only to "Kitty"—an appellation that was all right for a small kitten but is exceedingly ridiculous for the huge, shambling, rakehell, striped tomcat he has become. As he grew, he began to resemble a multitude of things and some people—sometimes he saunters with the gait of a grizzly, sometimes the heavy-padding, high-hipped prowl of a jungle cat; at other times he stalks with the absurd, Prussian prissiness of a German field marshal. And often, when he is dozing on the couch beside the fireplace with the v-shaped smile that sleeping cats wear, he looks for all the world like Winston Churchill. But since he attained his majority, he has never acted like a cat. It's unnatural and unsettling. He will not touch tuna fish, not even the all-white variety packed in water that we allow ourselves for special treats. Nor will he eat any brand of commercial cat food we've been able to find, except one overpriced and rare-as-black-pearls variety available in two ostentatious pet emporiums in the city. If he were a New York cat, he would shop at Gristede's.

He will eat coleslaw, hollandaise sauce, some kinds of ice cream, Stilton cheese, and once got into a pitcher of Bloody Marys we left uncovered and came rolling bawdily into a Sunday brunch drunk as a goat, with a rim of red around his lopsided smirk.

From his infancy, we could detect no vestige of emotion, feline or otherwise, in his entire makeup, except pained forbearance at having to depend on such as we for his livelihood and bursts of peevish malice at such good souls as the vet. The latter now greets us, when we come in with a carrier full of writhing, bristling yellow cat, with "Well, well, here's our big old yellow fellow again, huh?" This is followed by a persimmon smile and the drawing on of gauntlets similar to those a lion handler wears. Peter has been a frequent guest there.

No emotion, that is, until one strange, foggy autumn evening when I opened the back door and an enormous, gray, sloe-eyed Persian came ghosting in out of the mist as though he had been summoned. "Oh, no," said Heyward. "Uh-uh. That thing is somebody's familiar, and is not going to live here. No way." He did, of course; he became Major Grey, because he glided straight for a platter of cold lamb garnished with that august brand of chutney and demolished it, pronounced it adequate in his breathy Jackie Kennedy voice, and staked out his territorial claim on a brocade Chippendale side chair in the dining room. He sleeps there to this day. The Major is possessed of the greenest eyes, the most Madonna-like face, and the vilest disposition I have ever seen on a cat, and will not gladly suffer a fool. These things we learned later. On that evening, having fallen irrevocably in love with this exotic October creature, I chopped tuna and warmed milk and fluffed cushions and scratched under the velvet chin and was rewarded with a throbbing, thrilling purr. "Oh, Heyward," I caroled, "he's such a *sweet* cat. He's going to be such a joy." In the middle of the love feast, we had forgotten about Peter Quint, who was out in the night woods, looking for something slightly smaller than himself to slay.

A whump-whump-whump of the swinging cat door announced him. In he stalked, all restrained elegance and missionary demeanor. The quintessence of cool. The late George Apley. The Calvin

Coolidge of the cat world. And practically fell over the gray Persian, who was dining, Judas-like, from his dish. I have never seen such a sincere and heroic tantrum, animal or human, in my life. He behaved so ludicrously like an enraged, rotten-spoiled four-year-old that I actually expected him to hold his breath and drum his heels on the floor. In one sweeping, magnificent gesture, he swiped the startled Persian across his Chinese-empress nose, leaped, yowling his frustration and betrayal, onto my forearm and hung on, biting like a demon, ran up the floor-length drapes to the top of the valance, and crouched there, muttering in his throat, ears skinned back against his skull, looking for all the world like a cornered stoat.

He had achieved what the Esalen people call a breakthrough. At that moment, emotion came to Peter Quint. And war came to our house. Not once in the five years of their acquaintance have Peter Quint and Major Grey ceased hating each other, ambushing each other, mauling each other, making the nights hideous with sudden thundering, spitting, yowling sorties up and down the hall outside our bedroom door. We have come to view it as we do the Middle East—unlikely to erupt into the Big One and even less likely to cease.

The next pilgrim to seek sanctuary in Annie's Ark—a husband-spawned appellation I do not find amusing—was a cross-eyed, pregnant young cat so dreadful that she immediately became known as Miz Ugly. Even I could not truly love her, but I could not deny her sustenance, either. Happily, she was so frightened as to be nearly feral and wouldn't come into the house. She dined on the back steps and fled into the woods when I tried to approach her. But she did make us a gift of her kittens. There were two of them, brought neatly by the napes of their necks and deposited on the back porch on the day that Miz Ugly left us for some—I hope—more congenial haven. Two barrel-stave-ribbed, changeling kittens, one of whom we named Mildred Pierce because even then she had a Joan Crawford, hat-in-the-office manner about her, and one whom we named Jubal Early. I can't remember the why of that. He looked exactly like Disraeli, with a strange, long, hooked nose. The handwriting on the wall was swift and vivid this time; Peter and the Major would not tolerate this new territorial invasion, and the Middle East looked like it was gearing up for Armageddon. Sobbing, I crammed them into the cat carrier, and we drove them home to Fairburn to the truly tender mercies of my mother's maid, Nellie Arnold, a wonderful woman who was my infant nurse and teenage mentor and duenna, who would have accepted a pair of Bengal tigers if they had come from me. She took them home with her, where, I am assured, they flourish and hunt field mice blissfully to this day. (Being natural outcasts and Jonahs, I have a heart-deep feeling that Something has long since happened to them, but there is a conspiracy among Nellie and my parents to shield me from animal tragedies, and I will never know.)

Then came Gloria Mundi, so named because, while we had her, she never failed to get sick in transit to and from the vet's. Gloria was a Camille-like creature so slight and ethereal that we did not even realize she was in the family way until she had kittens under the bed in the guest room. Like Miz Ugly, she disappeared as soon as she had them toddling, and again there were two cadets in training for the Middle Eastern conflict. Before I could even form an opinion about them, Heyward had given Wednesday—the day of her birth—to his secretary, and we dispatched Charles Foyer (he took refuge in our flagstone foyer and lived there for three weeks) to the long-suffering Nellie. I am sure of Charles's fate—her young grandson dotes so on Charles that he is never out of his sight, and I see Charles often, with my own eyes. He is sleek and handsome and stately with, I think, a lot of Burmese in him.

Then, for a while, the procession of maladjusted fauna abated. For one whole summer, we were tranquil and creatureless. Oh, there was a demented turtle who lived in our front yard creek, who spent the whole of the summer ponderously plying his way back and forth between the creek and the shrubbery around the front door, like a witless tugboat. And two gentle, zebra-sized German shepherds and a fat, asthmatic one-eyed cocker spaniel thundered through our back yard every morning, with ports of call at our garbage can. But they were definitely Neighborhood and so were above suspicion. We had a remission.

And then the Time of the Possum began. It was in early December. My husband had gone out to pick up an order of Chinese food, and except for the sullen Peter and the choleric Major, I was alone in the house. I had started to think about Christmas decorations, and remembered that last year's assortment was packed away in the big walk-in closet of the then-unused back bedroom, which we called—accurately— the Dirty Room. It was a sort of warehouse for all the wicker and wrought iron I lived with in my single years, and the door was always kept closed for aesthetic reasons, as well as practical concerns, like heating costs.

Until we made it into a cozy, jumbled, warm den, I had never really liked that room. It is long and narrow and cavernous and vaulted and gabled, and it has tall, squinty, semi-Gothic windows that look out into the deep blackness of the woods. It was always full of small tickings and shufflings and creakings, probably only because it was cold and empty. But if you ran across that room in a Mary Roberts Rinehart novel, you would know immediately that this was where It happened many years ago, that the evil that emanated from the crumbling mansion, as jacket blurbs are fond of saying, had its source in this room. I always used to hurry past that poor, innocent room, where the two lovely people who owned the house before we bought it slept for thirty happy years. I would avert my eyes as though, if I really looked at it squarely, Something Awful would be leering back at me through the crack in the door that will never close squarely. The regrettable fact is that I am a coward and do not like being left alone in the house at night.

On this night, with a wild-eyed Peter Quint eeling around my ankles, I opened the door, reached in and flicked on the light, and proceeded resolutely to the closet. Sure enough, my shopping bags full of holiday cheer were there on the floor behind a pile of luggage, and I reached down to drag them out. And from the shelf above my head, just as I had always known in the custardy core of my being I would someday, I heard a hideous, sly, sibilant hiss.

It is absolutely true what they say about hair standing on end. Mine did, at the nape of my neck, and the nasty, crawling sensation is something I never care to experience again. I straightened up slowly and jerkily, like a marionette, and there, two feet away from my face, nestled into an old summer bedspread, with his legs tucked under him cat-fashion, was the largest, most unattractive opossum on all of God's earth. He grinned at me demoniacally with his too-many teeth and hissed like a teakettle. He looked for all the world like a lunatic collie. I ran.

I do not know how he—she?—got into the house, much less into that room, much *less* that closed closet, to say nothing of onto a shelf that is as tall as I am. It was, however, academic. Happily, the possum was still there, hissing and grimacing, when my husband came home and verified its presence. Otherwise, I'd have thought I was going 'round the bend.

How do you go about getting an enormous, hostile possum off the top shelf of your closet? You assuredly do not pick him up and remove him—not when he's facing you teeth-first with blood lust in his eye. We called the Humane Society. "I always heard you could get 'em by their tails," said the bored night watchman. Since ours was sitting on his, we had no opportunity to determine if this was fact or folklore. When we went back, the possum was gone. Of course, we didn't know *where*, but after looking under and behind everything in the house bigger than a bread box, we decided he'd gone out the way he came in, and went uneasily to bed.

That was just the beginning. For three years now, Parsifal Possum has been a fact of our lives. His usual ingress, we found, is the cat door. He sits on the back porch, staring hungrily through the kitchen door as though he wants to possess our souls. We have found him in the kitchen more than once, glomming up cat food. When he's shooed out, we hold the back door open for him, and he waddles out in a huff, giving us a beady glare of outraged hospitality over his shoulder. He trundles down the steps, out the flagstone path to the patio, and vanishes into the woods beyond. Sidney Greenstreet, departing in a fine pet, could not be more eloquent.

We find him frequently under the bed in the guest room, just sitting there—once, unfortunately, when my urbane parents-in-law were visiting from Washington. My husband's attempts to sweep him out with a broom are met with sublime passive resistance. I never saw a possum so hell-bent on living like people. I suppose he figures he's finally achieved the Good Life.

One evening not long ago, I found him in the kitchen again, eating cat food. I watched him for half an hour from the hall. Methodically using his front feet like horrid little hands, he picked up each dish and cleaned it out like a vacuum cleaner. He ate two bowls of Puss 'n Boots Gourmet Feast, one bowl of Little Friskies (Ocean Fish variety), drank a bowl of milk, reconnoitered every square inch of the floor until satisfied that no scrap or shard was left, and grumpily took his leave through the back door, which I held for him like a well-trained butler.

My husband's aside to the Orkin man has, I realize, a certain ring of truth. This onslaught of animal idiots is not the result of positive ions or a temperature inversion. My other animal-loving friends don't get an Oz-like procession of St. Francis's castoffs. I guess it's me. Any indigent unicorns may be directed to my house. There are enough Little Friskies for everybody.

Winter Island

One late-winter Thursday evening last year, I had a fight with my husband. It was one of the landmark bad ones, a bitter, vicious, wounding thing and the sort a man and woman don't get over. The words said during these mini-murders leave small, separate, pitted scars, as though acid had been thrown, buckshot fired. Sheer human ugliness leaves ineradicable soil and stains. These are not like the day-to-day wrangles and the running territorial skirmishes that thread any marriage. We survive our bad ones, but they remain on our hides. We are still us, but scarred and eroded.

I've forgotten what it was about or who started it or who won it—no one, obviously—but I reacted the way I nearly always do when I am hurt and sickened and outraged. I run. Usually, it is only to the office upstairs, or my hollow out in our woods, or to the car, to drive, sniveling, around town for a while. I had never quit our roof and bed. But I do run, physically. Part of my flight syndrome is cowardice at the prospect of raw confrontation. Part is guilt at my part in it. A great deal of it is a lower-animal instinct to get very far away from the fight, my antagonist, even the walls that contain and photograph the hurt. It seems to me at these times that the very air around us is thick and screaming and full of things that wriggle and teem and bite like bees. I also suspect that there's a large chunk of the three-year-old running away from home after a spanking in there somewhere.

At these times, I ache for flat, vast, still things and quiet. And so, when my friend Jenny called, hideously coincidentally, that evening while I was holed up in my attic lair, and said she was leaving her husband, I didn't sit down with a fresh cigarette and wait like an empty pitcher to be filled with her telephone-wired hurt. I said, "Throw some things in a bag and let's go to the island. Tonight. Right now."

"I'm going to St. Simons with Jenny," I told my husband, who was reading his own pain over *Wall Street Journal* print. "I will be back in a few days, probably. Or maybe I won't."

It was a near-mortal stab, and calculated to be so, and it got the only response it could have.

"Fine. Do whatever you like."

"You might remember to feed my cats. None of this was their fault."

My cats. Enchanting person I am, when confronted with the worst that is in me.

We drove the three-hundred-odd night miles to the island in a strange, canted shell—Jenny and I, who are ordinarily almost ludicrously close. We could not talk to each other. I was running from; she, indirectly, was running to. The island was a refueling stop for her. There was a man, there had been a man for a long time, and she would go to him and be with him always after this decompression. It had been a sad and manic marriage for her. She was exhilarated, thrilling like a stretched wire. She was talking too much. I was silent and frightened and wanted to go home. Having for the first time nothing to talk to each other about, we talked at each other, or rather she talked, and I watched the thinning headlights and, finally, only the flinty mean moonlight on the ribbon ditches of black-mirror swamp water along the road, and wondered what the hell I was doing here, and if I could get back.

We crossed the causeway from rusty, stinking Brunswick over the moon-gilt marshes and onto the island at 5 A.M. The low, bloody winter sun would not rise for an hour yet, but there was the luminous light that seems to haunt the marshes of Glynn County in winter or summer, in daylight or by night. We had both known St. Simons Island since our childhoods and needed no directions to thread our way through the black moss-canopied roads, through the gently shabby little white town, and out the beach road to the King and Prince.

The King and Prince is a flung-out old hotel so close to the water that, at high tide, the Atlantic licks the crumbling sea wall. It had been very grand once, though never the luxe bastion of the favored that the Cloister, over on neighboring Sea Island, has always been. Once, there were debutante cotillions and tea dances in the courtyard, and balls in the grand salon; Japanese lanterns bloomed over its celebrated olean-der walk, and slow, sweet coastal rituals flowered in its salons and dining rooms and peppering of hidden, jasmine-breathing terraces. Over the years, it slid into a shabby, dreaming sleep. People began to go to the air-conditioned motels along the beach road. Its patterned carpets grew stale and sour and blurred, and its waiters limp-coated, and its desk people small and surly, and its tiny rooms were perpetually damp and peeling in the heavy air stirred only by ceiling fans. I loved it fiercely then.

A few years ago, an uncommonly sensitive Atlanta real estate syndicate bought it and meticulously restored it to its former sheen, and it is once again the splendid lady it was. Indeed, *Esquire* recently applauded it as one of the finest "undiscovered" vacation places in the country, and the reservations from Ohio and New Jersey and Canada have flowed like wine since. Nevertheless, at midwinter it isn't crowded, so we each got a small room on an inner courtyard and locked ourselves in with our following demons and, surprisingly, slept till midmorning.

We had not really come to be together, only to have someone to touch twilight bases with. Twilight is a poignantly lonely time on any shore. So Jenny went her way into the soft gray day, and I went mine. She knows a wonderful collection of people on the island, a rich, yeasty bouquet of well-born, fourth-generation islanders, migrated artists and writers, blacks, shrimp fishermen. Her roots are there, and her ancestors. So she went inland, to drive the marsh roads and to walk under the live oaks, and to call, and I went out onto the beach to let the island wash over me.

I have been to St. Simons Island almost every

summer since I was born. It has changed—a few plush resort communities have come, and the shops are chic-er in the small square block of downtown that runs down to the municipal pier, and the lighthouse has been smartened up, and there are more restaurants. But it hasn't changed in some essential way I can't define but need deeply; I would know by the back of my neck if it had.

In the summers, it is the white of peeling board cottages on stilts along the eroding beach, the dust-pink of tabby foundations, the pearly ecru of crushed oyster-shell driveways, the spindrift gray of Spanish moss, the black-green and tomato-red of window-shrouding oleanders, the opalescent wheat of the lion-colored, wind-surfed marshes, the dirty tan of the sand, the foaming hazel of the sea. On burning, singing summer noons when the tide is creaming in full and there is nothing in the world but high sun and hot wind and wheeling gulls and you, knee-deep in the warm, running sea, it can make you drunk with joy. On fast-darkening twilight patios, when you are thrumming with sunburn and clean and still damp from a shower, in fresh cotton and on your second tall drink, it can steal away your workaday soul. Its dead-black, thick-warm, starry nights, its leaning moss tunnels, and its white, dead, old moonlight can make you believe in ghosts. There are many. The new morning light from the east on its marshes can break your heart.

That is its summer face. I went out onto a winter beach. These are no places to walk alone, not when you are feeling shabby and have run away from home. Wind that sang down sand beaches last summer hoons down corridors of an old, dead moon in winter. The sea that ran freshening before a hot blue wind eight months ago booms in cold and opaque and white with anger across two thousand empty miles. The figures in the distance that were, on solitary early summer mornings, a good-faced man and his manic Labrador retriever—who are they? What are they? I remembered, sickly, a story called "Oh, Whistle and I'll Come to You, My Lad," in an anthology of ghost stories I have. I missed my husband. I was frightened, and everything was twice as vast and empty as it had ever been before, and I went back to the hotel and sat in the gray underwater light of the library and read.

That afternoon, Jenny hadn't come in, and I rented a hotel bicycle and rode down the scraggy black road to the village. There were people along the way—year-round islanders sweeping their front porches, getting into cars to pick up their children at school, pulling into the Dairy Queen, walking to lunch at the cafés in the village, line fishing for crab off the pier. They seemed like stage characters in an oddly two-dimensional play, a mindless and monstrous charade. They didn't seem to make any noise. With the going of the summer sun, the island's colors had gone, too, and it was a Polaroid photograph of an island town. Gray for the sea and sky, white for the houses and gulls, black for the macadam road and the oaks, sticky Polaroid-fixative sepia for the marshes and the sea oats. Every summer, I nod and speak to whomever I pass on my island ramblings; that day, I did not dare. I was afraid they would disappear. Or I would.

Ghosts went with me, though, and they were very real.

It is an old island, and a bloody one. One of its marshes is called Bloody Marsh; the battle that established English supremacy in the Golden Isles was fought there against Spain in 1742, and they say that the marsh water ran red with blood as well as the setting sun. Bloody Marsh has its own resident set of ghosts, and it is up to you, if you wish, to believe in them. Many islanders do, and I always did. There are the ghosts of the Ebo Negroes too, who drowned themselves in the Frederica River where their slave ship from England disgorged them, rather than be slaves to the white men whose Sea Island cotton plantations they were destined for. They drowned themselves still chained together, and you can, it's said, hear their chains on certain nights when the moon is right.

Black muscle and blood built the languid grace that the old island still wears like a torn cloak, and my husband's ancestress, the English Shakespearean actress Fanny Kemble, is said by some unreconstructed islanders to have singlehandedly caused the defeat of the South in the Civil War by penning a book entitled *Journal of a Residence on a Georgia Plantation*, which was so inflammatorily antislavery that many Georgians of that day believed it caused England to refuse to aid the Confederacy. Mrs. Kemble lived for a while on nearby Butler's Island, and I have always loved having married into her family.

This day, however, she didn't bear thinking about. I maudlinly decided in mid-pedal that I probably no longer belonged in her family.

There is the ubiquitous lighthouse ghost, too—or, rather, ghostly footsteps that prowl the circular

stairs, heard but unseen for a century, at least. There
is the ghost light in the old Episcopal Christ Church
churchyard that flits from stone to stone. There is
Mary the Wanderer, who rides the dark island roads
on a silent-footed white stallion, searching for her
lover who drowned in the Frederica River more than
a century ago. The 1970s have a hard time on St.
Simons Island. The dead are so much realer there.
So many ghosts, and not all joint property of the
island.

I had my own ghosts for company. Three-year-old
me, clinging like a cocklebur at the top of the seem-
ingly endless slide that sat in the seaside children's
playground, calling down to the tanned young man
and woman who were my parents, "Just remember,
I'm just a little girl three years old." Solemn, dark-
eyed and ringleted me sitting under a beach umbrella
with my rose-and-gilt blond cousin Janet, in identical
dotted-swiss sundresses, drinking Coca-Colas, she
smiling sunnily at the camera, me scowling suspiciously. We were so unlike, yet dressed alike, and the
same age, that strangers always stopped to exclaim
over us.

Strutting, square, teenaged me and a friend,
strolling carelessly along the tide line, chatting in
stagily oblivious animation, tossing our hair in superb
affectation, aware on every square inch of burned
skin that binoculars from the Coast Guard station
watchtower were trained on us.

Me at twenty-seven, walking on a wild February
beach hand in hand with a man I had thought I loved,
crying because Winston Churchill had died.

Summers, house parties, weekends . . . thirty-five
years of me, and none of them any more substantial

than Mary the Wanderer. And the last ghosts, like fresh paint: my husband and me the summer before, playing like silly puppies in this island world that I was showing him for the first time.

Back at the hotel, Jenny was in the dim little bar that looks straight out over the shuffleboard court into the surf. She had brought a writer friend with her, and we sat long into the twilight and then dark, talking about things that didn't much matter. There seemed to be a pane of glass between me and the world. Finally, there was nothing outside the carefully mullioned windows but a white line where the waves were breaking, coming in. Facing the windows, I saw a small, perfect white triangle of sail come ghosting into the black square of the window, just beyond the tide line. I watched as it tacked back and forth, weaving eerily and horizontally, stitching its own white tracery along the lip of the black winter sea. I watched it out of sight. I didn't mention it. I did not know if it was real.

In the morning, I called home.

"I want to come home."

"I want you to come home."

Jenny would stay on a few days; her journey was just starting. I got into my car to drive back to Atlanta. And I thought about the island I thought I knew so well. Where nothing is real, what you have brought with you to that place cannot be real, either. Perhaps thirty-five years of me, of summer Anne, are dead and have taken their places among the island's ghosts, moored to that old earth and unable to leave it. Gone. And that is a disconcerting thought. But if it is true, then maybe that worst Anne, that killer of love and trust, winter Anne, is caught there, too. I hope so.

We will go back to the island, but I do not think we will go in the winter.

I'll Never Make It
in Camelot

There is, on the outskirts of Atlanta, a subdivision named Camelot. Although it is probably as inevitable as property taxes and zoning squabbles, that any sizable city have a Camelot, it gets my back up badly. Atlanta's official Camelot has a large, shield-shaped sign lettered in what passed in the developer's mind for Old English, and there is what looks to be a manatee wearing a diadem couchant upon it. (My husband suggests sourly it should have a pink plastic hair curler rampant, or maybe a power mower.)

I have never dared enter it, feeling fiercely protective of *Morte d'Arthur* and *Idylls of the King*. But I'm sure there's a Leodogrance Lane, a Merlin Manor, a Pellinore Place, and so on. It would follow. A suburban haven my husband used to inhabit in what he calls his Former Life, called the Ponderosa, has, to my sure and certain knowledge, a Little Joe Lane.

It is very fashionable, of course, to denigrate suburbia and all for which it stands. Everybody is a denigrator of suburbia, and the greatest of these are those who dwell therein. "It's because of the schools," a Levi'ed young labor lawyer who lives in Giggling Glen will tell you. "We're getting out of here as soon as we get the kids into Choate." Or Chapin, or Lawrenceville, or whatever. "It's all we could find when Charles was transferred," says the bright new girl at the League of Women Voters meeting. "We're looking for one of those great old places in town to do over."

I denigrated along with the best of them when we first began to look for a house. I had lived for eighteen years of my life in a small southern town, another four on a small southern campus, another eight in a pre-singles in-town apartment complex, and for one married year in a downtown Atlanta high rise. All had their quirks and drawbacks, but I was comfortable and quickly assimilated into all of them. What I would not be assimilated into, I announced to one and all, was a suburb. The kind with a name. The kind where Plans A-B-C-D were rotated on one street, Plans B-C-D-A on another, Plans C-D-A-B on another, and so on. The kind where the saplings and the TV antennas were held up with guy wires; where every third house had a raw mound running from house to street, advertising a sewer-line catastrophe; where, if you went to dinner and had more than one drink, you'd be lost and doomed to drive forever, like a twentieth-century Flying Dutchman, trying to get out.

The kind with vinyl clematis climbing up the mail-box.

So, when it became apparent we could not live in our two-room high-rise city apartment without getting a divorce or pugilists' noses from colliding in the bathroom, we began to look. "Close in to town," I said to the wise, pretty girl who came to show us houses. "Something with at least an acre, lots of woods and real charm, not far from Peachtree Road, maybe a creek, and—you know—bay windows and funny crannies and things, and a real dining room."

"Good wiring and roof and a dry basement," added my husband, "and freshly painted."

"*How* high did you say you were willing to go?" asked our agent, sorrowfully. But she is canny and experienced, and our lares and penates were smiling.

She drove us straight to it. First house. Close in. One block off Peachtree Road. Sprawling down a wooded hill, set far back into an acre and a half of hardwoods, starred with wild dogwood and flowering cherry. A long drive crossing over a creek. Old brick and red boards, with ivy climbing a round turret over the entrance, diamond-paned windows. Even a brick well with a peaky roof. Three levels, a stone fireplace you could drive a Volkswagen into, a glassed bay window, new kitchen and furnace. And, if we ate macaroni for a year, just barely affordable.

"We'll take it," I said before I was out of the car. And we did.

Our house was then, is now, and evermore shall be the joy of my heart. It is on a sedate old street divided by a wooded park, a street of sprawling,

two-storied, "undesigned" old houses kept mani-
cured and sparkling by their owners. Our neighbors
are gracious people who do *not* drop in in stretch
shorts and hair curlers for coffee, being, for the
most part, older than we and possessed of great
good sense. It is a neighborhood, not a subdivision.
I wouldn't trade my house for any one of the
$200,000 ersatz Cape Cods going up in Old Hokum
out on the river.

Nevertheless, I should have felt the first *frisson* of
latent maladjustment when my father, who is perhaps
the best title lawyer in the South and knows whereof
he speaks, finished our title search and said, "Did you
know your house is in about the first subdivision ever
established in Atlanta?"

On the first Saturday after we moved in, boxes
and paperbacks and unplugged lamps everywhere,
we were invited to a five o'clock cocktail party given
by old friends. Heyward, dressed and chafing, was
sitting on the one piece of furniture in the living
room, a sofa, which by sheer, horrible accident of
placement looked from the living room straight
down the length of the house to the back bedroom
door. I was in the shower adjoining the back bedroom, washing my hair. I could not hear with the
water running.

Late, stark naked, and dripping from crown to
instep, I burst out of the bedroom door into the hall,
just in time to hear him say, in a silly, high, sheeplike
bleat, "Why, here she is now, I believe." I froze like a
pudgy September Morn.

Seated on either side of him on the sofa, with a
clear shot down fifty feet of hall to me, were two
Ladies. In the best sense of the word. Gloved, hatted,

teacupped. And riveted. In our neighborhood, I found, it is the custom for neighbors to call on new-comers on weekend late afternoons. It is a lovely custom, one observed far too infrequently now, and deserving of far more than a newcomer looking like a shaved muskrat, slowly drenching the carpet, one arm upflung in greeting like the Statue of Liberty, otherwise stricken to stone. I put on my husband's filthy bathrobe, wrapped a towel around my hair, and crept in to join them. They were marvelous, perfectly charming, completely as though I had been Saint-Laurented to the teeth instead of robed in last year's yellow-ocher tan.

Later, we found their cards, gently laid beside a dead geranium on the foyer console. Where the card tray should have been. "That," I said later, still quailing with humiliation, "is as sure an omen as if it had come out of a sheep's entrails."

It was. No matter what we did, it attracted attention. Try as we might to slip unobtrusively into the serene tapestry of Vermont Road, we seemed to do things that better belonged in a carnival traveling the red dirt south out of a flatbed truck. Going out into the dewy morning to snip the glorious roses left by the dear couple who sold us the house, I slipped on the mossy brick steps and sprained my ankle. Loudly, with neighborhood-arousing shriek. Walking to the mailbox to get the morning paper, our first house guest put his foot through a decayed chink in our bridge. Loudly, with neighborhood-arousing shriek. We kept our three-month-old godchild one weekend and she had colic for forty-six of the forty-eight hours. Loudly, with neighborhood-arousing shrieks. Three dinner guests, on successive evenings, backed two wheels of their cars off the narrow 1930-built bridge and had to be rescued clangorously in the small hours of the morning by all-night wreckers, red lights spinning. My cats took to terrorizing the boxer across the way and the mannerly little Siamese next door. And most unpardonable of all, in our lavishly bird-feedered neighborhood, they slew birds by the score.

Two incidents occurred within the space of two weeks that first year, incidents which will live in infamy in my heart and, I am sure, in legend on Vermont Road. For we were surely the stuff of legend by then. The first was the Woolybuggar Incident. This took place one evening just before dinner, when we were sitting peacefully in the living room with an after-work martini. From the den just off the living room came a low, crooning, singularly lunatic sound that quite literally stopped my heart for a moment. We got to the den door just in time to see a formless, fuzzy, erratically darting *thing* scurry across the floor and under the sofa. Every fact, fallacy, and fantasy I had ever heard about rabid animals came into my head—that they make low, crooning, singsong noises, that they seek shelter in dark, inaccessible places, that they fear absolutely nothing and will attack anything. Since whatever it was was entrenched under the sofa and the only way to extricate it was to reach blindly under and drag it out, we closed the doors to the den and called the Humane Society. (We do a lot of that at my house.) They referred us to the Atlanta Police Department, and feeling silly but preferring that to rabies or rabies shots, my husband called. Pretty soon a car, blue light spinning and siren screaming at a hundred decibels, roared into the driveway and disgorged an enormous, grim-faced young cop, armed with a revolver and a billy club. "You folks had better stand back," he said. "They'll go for anything." He eased the den door open, crept over to the couch, drew his gun while I sobbed, "Don't shoot it, don't shoot it, just put it out!" and jerked the sofa away from the wall . . . to reveal a small, silky, honey-colored Pekingese, who was just about as frightened as any dog I've ever seen. The cop picked him up, fondled his ears, handed him over to me, gave us a hearty, that's-what-we're-here-for grin, and departed, gunning his motor several times. Eventually, we located the pup's owner; in the meanwhile, we had collected quite a little crowd of onlookers there.

The second incident occurred eleven days later, on a Sunday morning. My husband's four boys, small then, were visiting from Florida. Godlessly, Heyward decided to spend this Sabbath cleaning leaves out of the gutters and hollows of our roof. It is a very erratic roof, low at its overhang as a crofter's cottage, but soaring to dizzying, bastard-Tudor heights and crosshatched with ivy. Heyward, in sneakers and his tweed hat, propped the ladder against the gutter and ascended. He worked his way up about five feet. The dead ivy vines began to roll like a treadmill under his feet. The ladder fell into the liriope.

Prudently, he realized he would break his neck if he so much as moved. I was not at home. The boys were stair-stepped on the ground beneath him, staring with the same rapt fascination with which I have seen them watch *Lost in Space*. "Ricky," shouted my husband, "go inside and call . . ." He had been going to say our next-door neighbors, who remain rocks despite our foibles. But the boys had vanished in a yelping pack for the telephone.

And called the fire department.

Within three minutes, the Fire Chief's red sedan shrieked on two wheels into our driveway. Behind it, in full bay, came the longest, most potently scarlet hook and ladder unit in the city. Siren still screaming like a hundred *bel canto* sopranos, a dozen rubber-slickered men with ropes, axes, and God knows what else spilled out of the truck and swarmed up to the roof where Heyward sat, arms crossed, tweed-hatted, mottled with fury and embarrassment. Flicking nimbly up their own superior ladder, they bore him down like a life-sized Buddha. The boys had fled.

By now, every resident of Vermont Road who could walk was foregathered solemnly on our lawn. In utter silence. Heyward thanked the firemen. "Oh, that's okay," said one. "We were kind of glad to get out, tell you the truth. Sunday's always a dog."

Not on Vermont Road.

"What in the name of God did you *tell* them?" Heyward asked the crestfallen four wearily, after justice had been done. "Just that there was a man at 3767 Vermont Road who was hanging on for his life," sniffed the youngest. "Did you see, Dad? They even brought a tarp to cover the body. It was *neat.*"

I recalled this graceless incident to my husband at the end of last winter, when the horse spent the night in our basement.

He was a magnificent four-year-old bay gelding

named Friday's Child, and he wasn't an unexpected guest. He was a forgotten one.

My husband either went to prep school, college, or worked with one quarter of the population of the country, and sooner or later, they all write or call to say they're going to be in town for a couple of days and it would be nice if, etc. Now, I am a natural if sadly undisciplined and haphazard hostess, and so long as the battered Hide-a-Bed in the den holds up, I adore whipping up anonymous casseroles (sherry covered a multitude of canned mushrooms) and lingering late at the dinner table over brandy and do-you-remembers. We can accommodate, in varying degrees of comfort, any number of sleeping bodies, and so long as we can, and guests are not allergic to cats and late evenings, I wouldn't think of letting them repair to motels.

I do, however, require advance notice on horses.

This one was traveling east from Texas with a distinguished thoracic surgeon, a classmate of Heyward's, and his young daughter, who was going back to boarding school in Virginia and taking her horse with her. John is a graceful and thoughtful guest and called well in advance to see if overnight stable accommodations could be arranged for Friday's Child. There are a couple of boarding stables in the area, so we anticipated no problem.

The week before the entourage was due in was extraordinarily hectic. Both of us made unscheduled, overnight business trips out of town. The disposal gave up the ghost. I lost an elderly filling eating a Tootsie Roll and had to make a flying visit to the dentist. On the Thursday night before our guests were to arrive, the weather turned warm, sullen,

and foggy, as it often does just before our chilly
spring arrives. The fog was sticky, dense, and
immovable.

The next evening, with beds freshly made, early-
blooming daffodils glowing in guest rooms, and
nameless casserole gently burping sherry in the oven,
John called. The fog had delayed them; it would be
quite late when they arrived. That was fine, dinner
would keep.

It was close to midnight when the car creaked into
the driveway. Hurrying out to greet them, I heard
Heyward swear under his breath. I also heard an
unmistakable soft whicker from the enormous trailer
behind the car. A horse. Of course. We had forgotten
Friday's Child.

He passed, I think, quite a comfortable night in
our basement. Fresh pine straw hastily gathered
from the woods made a fragrant bed, and he traveled
with his own oats. John assured me that horses often
sleep standing up; I hope that is true and that he was
not sparing my feelings. Friday's Child seemed none
the worse for wear when, early the next morning, he
was led from the basement, minced daintily up into
his trailer, and wheeled off into the fog, Virginia
bound.

I have no idea what the nice man down the
street—the one who walks his Scotty at seven-thirty
every morning of the world—thought as he watched
a satiny, tail-switching rump roll out of our driveway.
I hope he figured the whole thing was some fog-
spawned mirage, but I don't think so. He lifted his
golf cap solemnly to the caravan, repeated the gesture
to us as we stood in the driveway, and continued
homeward, Scotty-powered. It was the very fact that

he turned not one patrician, silver hair that capped it for me.

"What do you suppose they *think* of us?" I wailed to Heyward over my shoulder.

But he was cleaning the stable and didn't hear me.

SPRING

Spring in Atlanta:
An Unabashed Love Story

At the sodden end of January, when tempers and faces are fusty with indoors, spring puts a tentative foot down in Atlanta. There's the first flush of yellow forsythia, polite as a poor relation, uncertain as a twelve-year-old at dancing class. The red flowering quinces follow, bolder and tougher, and a spiky daffodil or two, and perhaps a few suicidal camellias, made giddy by a spell of warm February treachery.

After them, the deluge. Spring—the genuine article, the full-time, live-in Atlanta spring, doesn't unfurl in slow, sweet ribbons. It comes in with ruffles and flourishes, a whoop of rowdy azaleas, battalions of tulips, a cannonade of dogwood. Small, fierce deployments—the little bulbs, the hyacinths and iris, the thrift and candytuft and pansies—overrun the precise bones of winter. The purple and white wisteria smother the last remnants of resistance with implacable benevolence. The city is secured within a week.

Nowhere is the incredible explosion of flower power so evident as in the venerable Northwest section of Atlanta. This small, cloistered wedge of residential real estate is the city's Kensington, Mayfair, Neuilly, Fiesole, rolled into one. We don't live in it; few people we know do. But we're close enough so that, with a few small, furtive detours, I can get to work through it. It never fails to restore my soul to drive through the Northwest after a teeth-jangling day at the office.

And in the spring, it's like taking a bath in flowers. The Northwest is proud, stately, furred with graceful age, totally insulated from the cheerful mayhem generated by the city's supercharged growth. Meandering streets are vaulted with fine old hardwoods, flanked with massive houses, cool as caverns, quiet with the silence that falls only in the *real* Camelots of this world. Lawns are enormous; great velvet vistas are *de rigueur*.

It is this depth, this foil of greenery stretching away, this panoramic space, that makes Atlanta's Northwest a springtime fantasia so rococo it's almost laughable, almost a Disney place. You cannot envy the gardens there—if such phalanxes of color rioting unashamedly mile after mile can be called such. To do so would be to emulate *Paradise Lost*: to aspire to deity status with, surely, the inevitable attendant tumble. Gardens here come swarming out of hillsides, surging up from creek banks, lapping at houses. They speak, not of yard men, such as people on my street have if they're fortunate, but battalions of gardeners, squadrons of Davey tree surgeons. Most of them, like the old houses they threaten to engulf, are infinitely longer on charm and spectacle than on careful planning. Atlanta has its share of pedigreed land-scape designers, but, happily, they have been content in the Northwest to let the careening scope and the puckish cant of the hills do their own designing. There are very few structured and witty bowers there. They would look absurd and nervous, like a kitten steering a Cadillac.

Particularly during the glorious two or three weeks in April and early May, when everything lets go at once, garden fever assumes the proportions of mono-mania. House-and-garden tours throng the Northwest like regiments of cavalry. People from hundreds of miles away make the dappled canyons next to impass-able. Tour buses grind through like Hannibal's ele-phants. Residents of the area do a moderate amount of "never again" muttering ("Habersham Road in May looks like Indianapolis in aspic," our token Northwest friend is fond of saying), but the muttering is underlaid with the smug pride of a parent for a beautiful child.

Northwest Atlantans carry on as if they invented gardens. What their gardens lack in linear innovation, they make up in livability. Atlantans use them as nat-ural extensions of their lives. They potter in them, toil and sweat in them, sit in them in the cool end of the fierce spring afternoons. They have meals and meet-ings in them, teas and tours in them, family reunions in them. They bow to society in them. Generations of Old Atlantans have courted in gardens all over the city, and not a few marry there. Beloved pets lie in state in countless family gardens, and every year a new crop of barefoot, towheaded young heirs appar-ent to the Northwest take their first steps, staggering after the tall, omnipresent gardener and his stable of wonderful gadgets.

Among the ranks of Old Atlanta—a nebulous term that can only be precisely defined if you are Of It—plants have a mystique all their own, almost an animus, and are treated with respectful affection. Fond relatives are just as apt to give a newlywed couple a cutting from the cherished Pride of Mobile that Grandfather planted for Grandmother when *they* were married as they are to give a piece of silver; and the youngsters, having learned to be garden-proud before they could walk, would probably rather have it. Veranda conversation at one of the old clubs dwells on a new rosebush as often as on a new Mercedes. Rivalry for the services of a particularly intuitive gardener is keen, sometimes to the point of bribery and larceny. These ploys rarely work. Loyalty among these paragons is taproot deep, though it is probably more a loyalty to the earth than the family: a territorial imperative. Plants are things to be lived with, treasured, savored; like children, there is delight in all their seasons, and they are lavished with love and discipline and plain dirt wisdom through all of them. One old gentleman, a silver-thatched aristocrat whose family helped build Atlanta back from the ashes of the Civil War, speaks to his favorite azaleas by name. He has raised and shown them for forty-five of his seventy years, he explains, and by this time he figures they should be on a first-name basis.

The difference between just a garden and an Atlanta garden is crystal clear to Atlantans, even if the logic escapes everyone else. It's a matter of splendor for service's sake, a sense of the fitness of form for function. Atlantans' cherished conviction that no one else knows how to *use* a garden is, perhaps, a naïve and insular point of view, but it is as inalterably woven into the native fabric as Coca-Cola and Georgia Tech and will endure just as long. An Atlanta matron, so the story goes, serving as a delegate to a national garden club conclave in San Francisco, toured a prize-winning plot in an elegant residential section of that worldly city. She looked on in tight-lipped silence as her hostess pointed out the wire sculptures, the modular planters, the reflecting pools, the rare specimens of exotic Western flora inset in smooth white pebbles like a surrealistic chess set. "That's no garden," sniffed the Atlantan, unable to contain herself. "That's an agricultural experiment station. Just imagine coming out in an agricultural experiment station!"

I neither came out in nor will ever have a garden like the lady in the anecdote (I know what it looks like, having toured it with a properly awestricken group one spring; it's an artless Eden of flowering fruit trees). But every spring, driving home through the green underwater twilight of the Northwest, I know precisely what she meant.

Some Thoughts on the Cute, Cute Fifties

This past April, gritting my teeth through the spell of Cleaning Up that shakes me annually like a demon terrier, I came upon a cardboard box in the attic that held my high school cheerleader's uniform. It was carefully tissue-wrapped and moth-balled, undoubtedly the work of my mother, who tends to preserve my castoff ceremonial garments as though they will be donated to a museum one day. I lifted it out; a yellowed white V-necked sweater with a monumental blue C on the front; a hideous, ankle-flapping corduroy skirt of alternating blue and white gores, satin-lined; a pinheaded blue felt beanie; blue satin tights gone brittle and frayed with age. There was a spreading reddish stain across that skirt that came, I remembered, from sprawling headlong into a sea of red mud at the apex of an abortive cartwheel one Friday evening. The sweater had a darker, rusty stain that was the stigmata of some long-forgotten hero's nosebleed when I hugged him after a victory. Even the socks—the long, thick ones you rolled down into salami-like cuffs around your ankles, just above the bump-toed saddle oxfords—were there. Brushing attic dust and warm, fond, sycophantic tears off my face, I took off my Levi's and sweatshirt and put them all on.

Creeping downstairs like a shy shade afraid to haunt my own house, I padded shoeless to my bedroom mirror. It gave me back a figure from a Poe masque. Swatched and shrouded in dingy, too-long corduroy and too-bulky white wool, a true specter looked back at me with frank fright. The uniform still fit, but the blank, stone-smooth, black-lipsticked young face that belonged above it, framed with a slicked-back ducktail, had been replaced with a face that belonged above tweed and turtleneck at the supermarket. It was grotesque, like a baby in a sequined jumpsuit, or a matron in a romper. "Sis-boom-bah," I whispered carefully to the image, doing as if by rote a viscerally remembered pirouette that showed a flash of shredding blue tights. *That* was truly terrifying, and I dashed into the den, where my husband was watching Howard Cosell, for succor.

By all rights, he should have laughed, but he didn't. He smiled and hugged me and said, "You look sweet. I'll bet you were a cute teenager."

Looking back, I realize that's just what I was. It was what we all were in the mid-fifties, we Revloned and duck-or-ponytailed young girls; were, or aspired to be. Cute. The word may sum up that generation of naïve nubility better than any word has ever evoked the young-femaleness of any age.

Not for us the beckoning comets of professional eminence, political influence, or even what the Victorians called "a brilliant marriage." Marriage, certainly, was the carrot that motivated the young donkeys, but the prospects of a brilliant one would have terrified us. Uniform anonymity was our Grail. There was not a fledgling Curie or Bernhardt among us, not a De Staël-to-be, not a cadet Stein, not an aspiring Great Beauty or even a magnificent courtesan. The natural, healthy amorality of the female young was buffed out of existence by the etiquette column in *Seventeen* magazine. Any hint of sensuality was instinctively sublimated into such strictured physical channels as the girls' basketball team, the drill squad, the majorette corps. And, of course, the cheerleading team. We necked, naturally, in a succession of our fathers' Chevies out behind the gym after sock hops, or on Bluebird buses coming home from out-of-town football games, but it was more ritual than ripening, and about as sexy as the matings of oysters. Even physical desirability had to be ersatz to be acceptable. A burgeoning bosom—a *real* one—was armored away beneath starched dickies. (Conversely, it was proper, if one was bosomless, to correct the oversight with dreadful, concentrically stitched affairs known as Peter Pan bras, as rigid and uniformly molded as those silver bullet-shaped projectiles on the bumpers of '51 Studebakers. Why this was okay and real breasts vaguely shameful I can't recall. Presumbly, an impressive cantilever was fine so long as it didn't jiggle.)

A pair of really fine, delicately hollowed cheekbones or a high-bridged Roman nose were afflictions second only to acne. To be tall was to be unclean. It was the era of the button-nosed, squirrel-cheeked, dimpled Cute Face. God, what we wouldn't suffer in the name of Cutehood.

An ordinary spring school day was a case in point.

My peers and I would get up at dawn for the rites of hairdressing. I to untorture the million tiny pin curls with which I tried—vainly—to subdue my thick, curly mop into a sculptured, fluff-fringed, side-banged cap; they to create helmet-smooth pageboys, perfect poodle cuts, or enameled ponytails with a rubberized circlet of artificial flowers where the tail met the pony. The nylon panties came next, and the ubiquitous, stabbing Peter Pans, then a layered assemblage of crinolines in various stages of flaccidity. After that, a starched sleeveless blouse with a high, military collar, centered by another clump of artificial flora, or a scarf. Over that went, almost to a maiden, a chain bearing an outsized class ring. A starched circle of skirt next; we had permanent abrasions at midcalf where all that starch and crinoline met leg. An elasticized cinch belt finished off the whole ensemble and often the wearer; our high school Phys. Ed. teacher once made an impassioned appeal in Friday morning assembly for this elastic foolishness to cease, since hyperventilating young ladies were passing out like flies in unair-conditioned halls and homerooms.

Then, on pinched bare feet, black kid Capezio shell slippers or pleated-toe ballet slippers. And on to makeup.

I can still remember the *maquillage* of the fifties. It was as formal and prescribed as a Kabuki dancer's. First a coat of Helena Rubinstein in rachel. Then polka dots of Cuticura to mask the hickies. Then a flouring of rachel powder that stayed rachel only until you worked up the day's first sweat, at which point it turned orange. Vivid, primary green or blue half-moons of eye shadow, if your parents permitted it. Black Maybelline mascara put on with spit and a

brush. Black Maybelline eyebrow pencil. And finally,
a thick paste of Fire and Ice lipstick if you were
brunette, Persian Melon if anything else. And a cloying squirt of Fabergé—Woodhue or Tigress—to min-
gle with all the Mum and Odor-O-No creams rising
steamily from stinging young armpits in homerooms.
Small wonder windows were kept open; wonder,
indeed, that this icing of drugstore Vilma Banky
could be considered Cute. But it was.

In fall and winter, the makeup stayed constant, but
the uniform changed. Hobbling wool skirts with a
rakish, two-inch side slit to display the obligatory lace
slip. Matched twin sets—cashmere if you were well
born, lamb's wool if you were not, quite; nylon given
to rabbitlike pilling if you were below the salt.
Starched white Peter Pan collars that fit under your
sweater neck and produced another garrotelike abra-
sion, or a single strand of pearls that came exactly to
your collarbone. The ring-on-a-chain or, in some
sophisticated instances, a college fraternity pin
poised dizzily on the left Peter Pan extrusion. The fat-
sausage socks (angora, one miserable, itching year),
and Bass Weejuns with a penny in them. It didn't
much matter about your winter coat; if you were Popular, you wore some young Clydesdale's letter jacket,
and if you weren't, no one really cared if you froze.
Least of all you.

Prom nights were occasions for exquisite, Torque-
mada-like torture. I don't know about the rest of the
country, but in the South, we wore, by God, hoop
skirts. They came in a round plastic box about the size
of a cake tin and consisted of three tiers of graduated,
expansible rings, which, when fully flowered, looked
something like the superstructure of a surrealistic

Christmas tree. These came next to last, however, just before your formal. First there was a three-hour celebration of bathing, oiling, shaving, talcuming, buffing, perfuming, currying, combing out, and the inevitable makeup. This was rendered prom-worthy by the addition of tarnished-gold or pewtery eye shadow and an extra helping of Fire and Ice, which would bleed gorily onto several rental tuxedo lapels by the end of the first "slow dance." Then lace-trimmed, Christmas-present panties, and slick, opaque stockings weeping ankle-ward from garter belts. (Frightful things, these, but I am assured by several men of my current acquaintance that those strapped and buckled devices were, and still are, the sexiest undergarment ever donned by women.) Then a truly terrible thing called a Merry Widow, another Peter Pan contrivance which came to midhip, pushed your bosom skyward (often augmented by another pair of stockings, to produce a chaste, linear cleavage), and required the services of your mother and your best friend to snap up the back. The legendary waists of the antebellum South had been hardened into young tree trunks in the fifties by field hockey and physical education, but at least twice a year they dwindled to near-Scarlett diameter.

Over this armadillo-like carapace went the hoop, extended into its full, *bibelot*-smashing circumference, and then the formal. Boned and strapless they were, of net or tulle, with acres of drifting skirts, often sprinkled with sequins or rhinestones, and they were infallibly pink, blue, mint green, yellow, or lavender. A net stole went along with most, as did dangling rhinestone earrings, a beaded evening bag, which would hold compact and lipstick but not your illicit Pall Malls, a velvet or bunny-fur jacket or your mother's fur stole. And silver or gold ballet slippers, since most of us were as tall as our dates.

You would clank like a pastel tank into your living room, unable to sit, propped against a handy mantel, until your date, unhappy and alien in tux and dangling, red-wristed hands and Vaseline Hair Tonic, arrived bearing a purple orchid or a funereal white posy of carnations. And then began the *opéra bouffe* of getting you into his father's car.

We double-dated then, by necessity, since few of our gentlemen callers had cars of their own, and those who did owned malodorous hot rods bared to the elements and entirely unsuitable for conveying a cargo of elephantine butterflies. One couple would already be in the back seat, he cowering against the door, she peering from an auto-filling, overrisen soufflé of skirt which her hoops had pushed up around her shoulders. I forget the precise technique for getting into a car in a hoop skirt, but it involved raising the whole affair to waist level behind and sidling in sidewise. You would not, of course, expose your behind to your date, so you shone your panties toward your own front door. I have more than once heard my treacherous father chuckling as I departed for a prom.

My musings on the Cute, Cute Fifties did not include, this spring, any thought as to the wherefores of them. It was, to me, a strange, muffled, frightened, smug time, perhaps more so in the South. Somehow the tenor of every age seems to be intensified into caricature in the South. I don't remember having a very good time during the fifties, though I certainly thought I was at the time. Perhaps it was because, in the core of my soul, I never achieved true Cutehood, though I did the walk-through faultlessly.

I leave the tenor of those times to Peter Bog-danovich and Dan Greenburg, who have caught them exquisitely, though, as Dylan Thomas said wistfully of the wasp book he received on one of his legendary Christmases in Wales, they told me everything I wished to know about the fifties except why.

But the powerful magic of Cutehood lingers on. It must. Recently, a friend gave a costume party. And seven women came in their high school cheerleaders' uniforms.

My Grandfather Died

∞

On a sweet, windy, green afternoon late last April, my grandfather died in the hospital in Newnan, near the farm that had been his home for seventy of his ninety-one years. It was his kind of day; it had been a week of his kind of days, and on one of them, he had shot his .22 rifle at a crow who was dive-bombing the young fruit trees in his orchard a quarter of a mile away, and had been keenly distressed because he had only winged the crow. More than just about anything in his gentle life, he hated to hurt an animal. He killed living things only when they directly threatened the growing things that were his livelihood, and then in silent, sorrowing misery.

I was deeply sad for his ended life, but sadder for myself and my father and aunt and the tart, tough, strong little countrywoman who was his wife, who became misted and shadowed and vague after he left, as though he had been the deep-rooted Maypole for her volatile, antic, dancing life.

To say he was a man of few words is to put it ludi-crously mildly. She was the talker in the family: the one whose temper flared, whose glinting impatience whirled into sudden, grandchild-scattering storms, whose florid rural sayings and adages are even now legendary in the little town where my family has lived for five generations. "You look like the hind axle of bad management," she would tell me when I came moping and scuffling around in the throes of some unrequited, fourteen-year-old passion. Or, on the eve of my departure for Europe: "I don't like it, you over there running around with foreign Hottentots." Her explosive "God knows!" invariably signaled an epic ouster: bothersome grandchildren from her pantry, flapping, hysterical red chickens from her vegetable garden, assorted barnyard cats and an endless succes-sion of white spitz dogs from the dairy barn or the mule corral. She had a magnificent streak of thespian in her, a mile wide, and employed it shamelessly and with relish. If you had known my grandparents only slightly, you would have picked her for the strong one.

But it was Dad Rivers who was that, strong with the strength of a willow rooted deep in his red earth, not only capable of bending with her storms but becoming glorious with them, as a willow is most beautiful tossing back the hubris of a windstorm. "Clyde," he would say to her when he had had quite enough, "that'll do right well." He rarely said it, but she subsided into a sort of dark, stormy quiescence that was exotic and lovely when he did. They comple-mented each other like earth and fire, and loved each other always.

I never knew a man more of the earth. He farmed

it, never making much money for his cotton and corn and oats and his bursting, jeweled vegetables, but never owing a cent to any man, either. Until my father bought him an ancient jury-rigged Ford tractor (which became the unadulterated joy of his heart), he farmed with a succession of stately mules—Alec and Jane are the first ones I remember, but there were others before and after, tall and glistening and frosty-muzzled. He was a great connoisseur and under-stander of mules, and they would obey docilely his soft, drawled "gee, haw!" in the fields when they would obey no other human being. Indeed, I think my grandmother disliked those mules as much as she did Republicans and shiftless people, for the simple reason that they were about the only living entities who would not knuckle to her—but would practically purr for Dad Rivers. The only time in my life he was ever crisp with me was when he caught me sitting on the corral fence shooting Duck Legs—a mean, ear-skinning troglodyte of a yellow mule whose name was exceedingly graphic—with a BB gun. "That's enough, Sybil Anne," he said. The "Sybil" was the tip-off. Whenever I was in trouble as a child, I knew it by the inclusion of my first name.

When I was very small, I thought he could talk to animals. I mean a two-way conversation. In some earth-simple, arcane way, I still think he did; wild things would come and eat out of his hand. My father swears a red fox did, once. He probably talked more to them than to people. And when he talked to people, it was usually about animals. "Martins are late this year," he would say to my father as they stood, hands in pockets, staring up at the tall pole with hollowed gourds affixed to it which he had put up for a winter hotel for the martins. He liked to watch them wheel and dive in the mauve of an autumn sunset, and late or not, they always came.

"Bream ain't likely to bite if you wiggle your feet in the water," he would tell a squirming, bored, barefoot me when we were fishing with crawlers and bamboo poles in the pond where the creek ran into the calf pasture. We could sit for hours in the pearly summer mornings or evenings, fishing, alone together and absolutely silent. A child doesn't feel uncomfortable with silences like an adult does; I learned early what deeps of unsaid words were in his, and we were comfortable in our skins with each other. I cannot maintain precisely that same depth of quiet with any other adult I have ever known, but the knowledge of its existence is, along with the unspoken pride and love I know he always had for me, his best legacy.

He could read a bad winter infallibly in animal fur and lichens. He knew in February if the potato hill in the side yard would produce firm or rotted fruit the following autumn. Earth and sky spoke to him as they never will to me. My father has it, this near-mystic kinship with elemental things, but I think it skips girl children. I know that he burned inside with joy and bemused wonder when I was chosen valedictorian of my senior class, when I went away to college, when my first byline appeared in a magazine, though he would only say, "Well, Anne, that's real fine." But I think he was closest to me when I knelt, transported, over the wriggling armful of white spitz puppies produced semiannually by Easter Ruffles, or a fragrant new calf, or a ridiculous, bubble gum–pink Disney piglet. The bond we shared then was palpable and old as the world, and needed no cluttering words from inarticulate man or child.

His patience is a family legend, and its finest hour was when one of his best milk cows, an obtuse Jersey named Dora, escaped from the pasture and disappeared. My father, my uncle David, my two cousins, and I, all of us, turned out. The loss of a milk cow was a financial disaster to the farm and a personal agony for Dad Rivers. For three days, we searched woods, fields, along the highway and railroad right-of-way, on neighboring farms. My grandmother fussed and chirred in her kitchen as suppers grew cold, waiting for the flashlights to come bobbing home, growing more vocal and exasperated. On the evening of the third day, we found the place where Dora had gotten out: the barbed wire that skirted the edge of a deep, red-clay overhang along a dirt road that bisected the farm was down. Shortly after that, we found the cow, and it was Dad Rivers who led the witlessly lowing, bursting-bagged Dora home to be milked, with just a hand on her muzzle. Supper spoiled again, my grandmother started her Greek chorus of raillery at dumb beast and man alike. Dad Rivers would have none of it. "She ain't roguish, Clyde," he said mildly but with iron in his voice. "She just fell out of the pasture."

I remember so much about him—the trips to the gristmill in the laden wagon, when he let me take the reins of the twin harness wherein Alec and Jane twitched mellowly down the red road. The faces and baskets he used to whittle out of May's green may-pops. How he could bring down a fine branch of mistletoe with one deft .22 shot. Yates apples from a basket beside the fire in the bedroom where we always sat, which he would toss me wordlessly when I grew bored with grown-up talk. A reddened, splayed, gentle hand putting kerosene on a nail puncture, or a wad of well-chewed tobacco on a bee sting. His thin, stooped, sturdy figure returning down the road from Ginn's store with a pocketful of Hershey's Kisses along with the bread and baking powder and fertilizer. What those diverted pennies must have cost him I never thought about, but they bought him a lot of me, and I suppose he counted them well spent.

When he died, he lay in an open casket in the funeral home, as is the custom in my part of the South, and I was surprised at the people who came by to see him. City-born people inevitably think this a grisly rite; it is not. It is the way we do it, and he would have found anything else unthinkable. Half the county was there, and if there were tears, there were far more fond and amused and loving anecdotes about him, far more things to celebrate and cherish, far more to respect. People who had known him dropped by to check in with him one last time; people who hadn't known him but knew my father and Aunt Grace came, instinctively knowing a loss such as this must not go unmarked, that a man such as this would not be born again in a changed world. Even my own peers from Fairburn, who knew only me, came. I had thought he belonged only to us; he belonged to a lot of people, it seemed.

I miss him rather abstractly, and only in spurts, for he was an old, old man and it had been, by his lights, a truly good life. Physically and temperamentally more a dark-eyed, flickery-mooded child of my grandmother than of his, I nevertheless am proudest when, having scooped up yet another roadside stray or fed another frowsy raccoon through a winter, my father says, "I know just where you got that."

I hope my grandfather knows, too.

The Baby Bachelors and Other Stories

One long, yellow spring day last year, my husband and I were semi-entertaining four of my former roommates who go back a long way with me. There were assorted husbands and dates draped slothlike on the antique lawn furniture on our infinitesimal brick terrace, and a sweating pitcher of orange blossoms, and torpid cats, and the good, sunny, sleepy smell of warm grass and three o'clock on a spring Sunday. The talk was comfortably anti-vivacious and a little silly, and only enough fat, irritable wasps to keep us animate left their headquarters in the liriope to strafe the orange blossom pitcher. Everybody knew everybody and was easy in the knowing, and it was a very fine spring Sunday indeed.

"Do you remember the Magnificent Mooch?" said one of us who had shared the singles-days ménage à quatre in one of Atlanta's most venerable and populous apartment complexes. We all remembered. "I never saw him without a glass in his hand," said

another of us. "It was never his glass," said a third.
"Or his booze or his ice cubes or, for that matter, his
apartment you saw him in," added one tall, pretty ex-
roommate who had burnt her Sweet Briar–fresh fingers rather severely on the Magnificent Mooch in the
first halcyon days of our emancipation from school.
"I dated that dingbat for one whole summer, exclu-
sively, and we left the premises exactly once, and that
was to pick up his laundry three blocks up Peachtree
Road. In my car."

"And then there was Tinker and Evers and
Chance," I remembered, and everybody laughed, but
not very hard. Tinker and Evers and Chance lived in
the corner apartment in our building and were, at
least to our eager-to-be-jaded eyes, urbane and
charming in the extreme. They were varnished by
that most rare and precious of patinas, Experience,
being then in their late twenties. One—Evers, I
think—was Over Thirty. Tinker and Evers and
Chance had an uncommonly tasteful and opulent
apartment compared to those of most of the young
men we kept company with—i.e., a rolling walnut
bar, an original, if hideous, oil painting, lined drapes
that came to the floor, ashtrays that didn't have the
names of hotel night clubs on them, a nice little collection of bric-a-brac for shelves and tables, a white
extension telephone in the upstairs bathroom, and no
wrought-iron bookcases or melamine dishes.

They also had a highly effective system whereby
they preyed upon the newly graduated ewe lambs
who moved into the apartment complex. (Whenever
they saw a moving van, they salivated, one sharp-
tongued friend puts it.) Tinker would cut a promising
one out of the flock and dazzle her within an inch of

her young life with dates every evening for a month or so. (Always in the opulent apartment and always, very properly, in the admiring and dateless company of Evers and Chance, which gave her a heady, Sweet-heart-of-the-Squadron feeling.) When another gaggle of ewe lambs moved in, he gently passed her on to Evers, who, in a month or so, relinquished her to Chance in favor of Tinker's fading new favorite. By this time, the original ewe lamb was so enamored of the group in toto, and so overwhelmed by the ambience of the Apartment, that she couldn't have cared less who squired her, as long as she remained a part of the magic circle.

For Tinker and Evers and Chance really were extraordinarily attractive and truly charming and had the rare and gentle quality of making you think you were quite the most marvelous thing in Capri pants. And they were never unkind. They were simply bone-lazy. All four of us original roommates had been the Tinker-to-Evers-to-Chance route, a process which occupied the better part of a year, and only after we had all been phased out and replaced by a new cycle of innocents did we become a shade testy about them—an opinion we found afterward that we shared, like a fifty-mission crush, with half the veteran females in the apartment complex.

Then, and only then, did we realize that the dinners for four we had in turn shopped for and cooked in that apartment would have catered a small airline, and that the little decorative touches we lovingly added to their domicile, along with those that had been bestowed by the lambs before us, could have made a showplace of Tobacco Road. I figure that roughly seventy-five women now living in the Greater

Atlanta area have been Had by Tinker and Evers and Chance, and I do not mean carnally. Whatever became of them I do not know, but while it was in flower, theirs was one of the truly creative and sybaritic regimes on earth.

"Where are the snows of yesteryear?" droned my husband acidly. I think such talk as we four were indulging in that afternoon makes most husbands fairly furious. But women, especially well-thirtied married women who were twentyish single women together, turn to the flora and fauna of those days with great affection. All the viciously lonely and dull times—and there are many of those—have faded along with the apartment-pool tans, and what is left is a brilliant tapestry of the titillating, the absurd, the funny, and the fun. We four are not now and never were exceptional, but we are convinced to a woman that the unattached men we knew then were unique to the point of being clearly defined social phenomena.

Some really were. Along with the common house sponge, like the Magnificent Mooch, and the creative and dedicated bachelors, like Tinker and Evers and Chance, our apartment complex was the official Valhalla for a species known to us as the Baby Bachelors. I understand that this hardy species still flourishes in precisely that same group of apartments and has spread to certain of the newer pleasure domes around town devoted to the exclusive nurture of Singles. Possibly the ones that live now in our old apartments are the selfsame ones we knew. Baby Bachelorhood is a career not to be lightly tossed away for anything less than a magnificently turned ankle firmly grounded in a grassy plot of inherited IBM stock. Endurance is, in fact, the essence of it.

Your average Baby Bachelor is somewhere between thirty-five and forty. Younger bachelors do not qualify, nor divorced men. One or two of ours were over forty, and the dean of them all was a battle-scarred rogue male of fifty-one. All of them seemed to have come from small towns in Georgia or North and South Carolina—we had a preponderance of South Carolinians—with a sprinkling from Tennessee. No Alabamans, though—Alabama-born BB's, I suppose, went to Birmingham or somewhere after college. All of them went to a military school or their state university. All of them belonged to a fraternity (one of the larger and more socially oriented brotherhoods), drank warm bourbon and Coke from Dixie cups on hot football Saturdays, and threw up behind the fraternity house around nine-thirty that evening. They called their elders "sir," be they deans, alumni, or the toothless operator of the campus gin mill and bawdy house, referred to their peers as good old boys (Tom Wolfe didn't invent *that*), maintained a Gentleman's C-average, and never got over the whole thing. Most of them can still, a quarter of a century later, give you the old fraternity grip—and do.

They wore their fraternity sweatshirts whenever possible and kept the decals on their Pontiacs and Oldsmobiles blazing bright. Most of their real estate and life insurance sales were made to their wistful counterparts who had somehow slipped up and married a homecoming queen or cheerleader in a fit of bourbon and Scott Fitzgerald in their senior years. They played endless games of volleyball in the parking lot in winter, water polo in the apartment pool in summer. I suppose that now they jog—in flying wedges. They went in jocular, boozy shoals on chartered buses

and trains to their homecoming games, and on game-
less Saturdays they drifted, sweatshirted and ingen-
ious, from female door to female door, empty glass in
hand, for a refill of whatever the lady had in stock. We
once gave one of our BB's cooking sherry. He didn't
seem to notice.

When they dated, it was in a group of their fellows. Their girls were usually much younger, homesick still for their own undergraduate cocoons. They
would go to a steak place with a piano bar, where one
of them would get into an altercation with a lonely
and truculent traveling BB from the Big Ten, who
wanted to sing "We are from I-i-i-o-way" instead of
"Glory, glory to old Georgia." When they didn't date,
they washed their cars.

I suppose that this present generation of collegians
will not produce many Baby Bachelors, being largely
caught up in Issues and grim-visaged war and pot
rather than ritual grips and homecoming and warm
bourbon. It's too bad. The world will probably be the
richer for them, but not-so-young girls in their summer dresses on some distant, dappled May Sunday
will be infinitely poorer.

Her Ladyship Regrets

∾

On the Friday evening of the long Memorial Day weekend last year, my husband came home with a December 1937 issue of a homemaking magazine, which he had unearthed from the potential holocaust that serves his office as a stockroom. It was totally enchanting, a pilgrimage back to a simpler, sweeter Christmas than this next one portends to be. There weren't the stupendous, glossy artilleries of color spreads that shout and boom at you from the pages of modern women's magazines, frightening you out of your wits and intimidating you into inferiority complexes. Instead, there were Kewpie-doll, candy-box ladies in the soft-slender style of James Montgomery Flagg doing homely holiday things like helping a child string cranberries for the tree, roasting huge, glistening, never-frozen turkeys in the ovens of coal ranges, directing the household servants in the laying of the holiday board. Servants? It was a long time ago.

Tucked away in the back of the magazine was a

little column, obviously a monthly affair, in which a
lady named Frieda Eustace Dean counseled fledgling
homemakers. Frieda Eustace Dean was apparently
the Heloise of her day, less terrifyingly jolly, but the
same sort of Delphic sybil, dispensing genteel chides,
folk wisdom, homely hints on the solemn responsibility of womanliness, and graphically practical instruc-
tions in such nonplusing areas as making your own
family dentifrice and soap, and how to make flypaper
last longer. In this particular issue, she was intoning
sweetly on the arts of ladyhood. Modern young
women of 1937, she said, could indulge in all manner
of emancipated peccadilloes, such as marcelling their
hair, smoking, drinking one or two pink ladies or
sherry flips, and wearing trousers à la Marlene Diet-
rich—*if* they were proficient in four basic feminine
areas. These were furnishing the home, gourmet cui-
sine, gardening and flower arranging, and sewing a
fine seam. Lacking these four basic assets, or even
one of them, you had about as much chance of
achieving ladyhood as a razorback hog in Tiffany's.

I must have blanched when I read it, because
despite my efforts to conceal the magazine under a
sofa pillow and divert him with Bavarian fudge ice
cream, my husband retrieved it and read the column.
He howled with glee. It seems that no matter how
one embellishes what gifts and talents I do have,
none of those four are in my repertoire. I've flunked
the ladyhood test, and may Frieda Eustace Dean fry
in hell.

Furnishing the home, I am convinced, is something a functional cretin can accomplish with her
feet, *if* she is content with wrought iron, laminated
plastic, stick-down carpet squares, and those prints

of kittens wearing aprons and firemen's hats that you can order, four for a dollar, in certain non-glossy publications. But I suspect that what old F. E. Dean had in mind was that subtle, elusive charisma known as Innate Taste. Innate taste means, to me, a compound of limitless time, lots of charge accounts, several years' traffic with the delicately vicious art of antique-spotting, and a decorator about whom you know something nasty but haven't told a soul—yet. Sour grapes? You bet your bottom Queen Anne splat.

By age thirty, through several years of apartment living with assorted roommates and one with a husband, I had developed a rather cavalier approach to furnishing the home. In my single days, couches were Christmas presents from compassionate parents, chosen for their ability to accommodate a running series of multisized fathers, brothers and lovers, and overnight guests with a minimum of sagging, rather than for style. Coffee and end tables ran to Formica, slate, or whatever an overturned Black Russian wouldn't mar. Carpets were hideous brown-and-white tweed affairs courtesy of the management, as impervious to cigarette burns and large, muddy after-football-game parties as corrugated iron. And about as lollable-on. When I graduated to my first married apartment, the management had provided parquet flooring and paneling, a great improvement over my brown-tweed era, and my decorating expertise expanded to potted palms in corners, a few good, if frankly stolen, original paintings from artist friends, and some welcome wedding-present bric-a-brac.

But when we moved into our house, desperation settled in. There are so many forbidding coves and nooks and spaces in a house that need filling—not, you know full well, with a wrought-iron telephone stand or a potted palm or inflatable couches, but with amusing, original, and spectacular things that prompt your friends to bubble, "It's so *you!*" Wrought iron is not me, though I am not quite sure what is. But originality, wit, and spectacle, I discovered, cost a veritable fortune.

So, during those first few barren-roomed weeks, I thought perhaps I'd better substitute a few choice antiques for wit, spectacle, and originality. Those were the innocent days when, to me, "antique" meant either a great aunt's fumed oak hat rack with ball-and-claw feet and a twelve-point buck's antlers for the hats, or the exquisite little Hepplewhite side chairs and the five-pound Lowe-stoft tureen that you ran across in mint condition, except for a little romantic dust, at a garage sale given by a senile, aristocratic little old lady. I was rudely cast out of Eden when I bustled into the Connoisseur's Gallery of a local venerable department store and blithely asked to see something in a Queen Anne tea table. Taking in my wrap madras kilt, cotton shirt, and sneakers, the chatelaine said, "We have a lovely piece for around two thousand dollars, dear, but some of our reproductions are quite charming. They're down on the mezzanine." So much for Frieda Eustace Dean's First Law of Ladyhood. I fled home and watered my potted palm. Things are better around here now, or at least the house is fuller of furniture, but last weekend, at dinner, our one by-God-*real* Chippendale side chair, a gift from my husband's lovely mother, collapsed in mid-moussaka under a guest. Being a friend, I don't think he's going to sue.

Gourmet cooking is another washout. I can get a

passable meal on the table in a reasonable length of time, thanks to canned mushrooms and Stouffer's frozen fantasies. But exquisite, candlelit little dinners for eight, with amusing centerpieces of Waterford *bibelots*, frankly terrify me. I subscribe to *Gourmet* magazine and read every word of it, vicariously presiding over other people's Dover sole–laden tables, and I clip hundreds of recipes for beef Wellington, *oeufs en gelée*, striped sea bass with sauce *verte*, veal Prince Orloff. So far, all they do is skitter out in a glossy white shower when I open my *Good Housekeeping Cookbook* to refresh my memory on beef stroganoff. I do have one specialty, a viscid, clottingly rich creamed tuna fish casserole that inevitably stupefies dinner guests into a coma. It's been the rounds of our friends, though, and like a fifty-year-old two-hundred-pound female relative in a wet suit, it can't masquerade as anything else. So we stick to shish kebab now. Once I did spend all day making a quiche Lorraine from absolute ground-zero scratch. It looked like a cheese-covered inner tube. Nobody knows how it tasted. Even the gluttonous cats took one sniff and fled.

Gardening and flower arranging? Last spring, I planted some caladium bulbs and waited all summer for them to emerge in glory. When they didn't, we dug. They were flourishing like the green bay tree— upside down, on their way to China. And when my mother gave me a clump of pansies in an earth ball, one of us, who shall be nameless, lovingly prepared the soil and planted the clump. The whole ball. My tomato plant produced one lone, grotesque, elephantine tomato. Thank heaven that only God can make a tree.

That leaves sewing a fine seam. In shortening a cocktail dress recently, I painstakingly sewed the front of the silk lining to the back, producing, inside the dress proper, a sort of glorified silk potato sack. At least I got a new dress out of that venture. But I don't recommend it as a habitual maneuver.

There is, as my husband says consolingly, more to being a lady than meets the terrible, swift eye of Frieda Eustace Dean. But it seems to me, a four-time loser, that the only lady who can achieve that kind of distinction is the kind you find in *Burke's Peerage*.

Thank God that, in these days of the Movement, it doesn't matter.

Tornado Weather

Ever since I watched *The Wizard of Oz* from beneath my theater seat, I have been terrified of tornadoes. They figure in my worst and most baroque dreams, those terrible reverse towers snaking down from flat-edged, flying clouds. I once slept through one when I was very small, while my mother and father sat beside my bed, ready to snatch me up and run for the basement if the hundred infernal locomotives howling through the night sky outside should dip toward our house. They did hit, a block away, in the black section of our little town, called, for some obscure reason, Lightning, and did fearsome property damage to the people who could least afford it. Three blocks away, a woman died when her bedroom ceiling crashed down on her.

I know what the Freudians say about tornado neuroses, and for all I know, they might well say it about me. But I know also that mine is a terror born as much of the dread of nameless malevolence and first-hand knowledge of death and destruction, as of some cosmic phallus. *Cosmopolitan*'s centerfolds don't frighten me. A funnel cloud does, to the point of nausea and senselessness.

On the same Memorial Day Friday that Frieda Eustace Dean came into my life, tornadoes came to town. And stayed the weekend. Atlanta was under a seventy-two-hour tornado alert. I was a walking, seventy-two-hour nervous breakdown.

Late March and April is their territory, and I had suffered the spurts and spats of wind that came then, the flattened mobile home parks on the evening news, the strewn tree limbs and power lines with my usual nervous, graceless prowling. May-going-on-June is *wrong*, though, for those screaming maenad winds, and the unnatural eeriness of the timing bothered me almost as much as the yellow-eggplant air and lashing trees. I don't like unseasonable weather. It makes me feel as though Armageddon is at hand, and me nowhere near a state of grace.

We had planned to go to a movie that first Friday evening, but "the possibility of tornadoes and severe thunderstorms" on the TV's sweeping radar screen suddenly changed to "Atlanta is now under a tornado watch. A funnel cloud has been sighted near Carrollton, sixty miles to the west of the city, and is moving toward the metropolitan area. Stay tuned for further bulletins and be prepared to take shelter should the necessity arise."

The necessity had arisen for me when I heard the first "possibility" bulletin. Shelter to me does not mean my friendly neighborhood mini-cinema. I do not wish to die with four hundred strange people who smell like popcorn and Milk Duds. Shelter to me is home, or, more precisely, the room behind our regular basement, half carved out of earth, with shoulder-high cement walls. It holds an old refrigerator and the skeletons of whatever small creatures the cats take there for their slow, formal waltz of death by torture. For this reason, we call it the Killing Ground, and, lit by the classic dangling, naked light bulb and smelling of damp earth and whatever I have unwittingly left in the refrigerator, it is unattractive in the extreme. On Tornado Days, it is beautiful to me. We did not go to the movie.

My husband refused to let me go and sit in the Killing Ground, much less go and sit with me. "You'll have plenty of time to get down there if anything hits, which it won't," he said. "You'll see the funnel long before it gets near." I was sitting on the arm of his chair and would have been in his lap if the craven Persian hadn't already been there, his pretty sphinx face buried under Heyward's arm. Major Grey was trembling as if in an ague, and I was drinking neat J&B and crying.

"You don't see funnels if they come down right on top of you, you idiot," I hiccuped, both from Scotch and terror. "You just hear a roar like a hundred freight trains and—"

We heard a roar like a hundred freight trains. The sky went from purple to green-black, like a rained-on oak tree, in an eye-flick. Trees outside the den windows bowed down to meet the ground. "Who has seen the wind?" I heard myself chanting thinly, absurdly. "Neither you nor I. But when the trees bow down their heads, the wind is passing by. Who has seen the—"

"*Will* you shut up?" said my husband.

What looked like a very large rhododendron went flapping levelly by, like a green, mutant pelican. The lights went out. I was rooted as firmly to the arm of Heyward's chair as Lot's wife.

It *was* a tornado, but fortunately it missed our street and nipped down perfunctorily a couple of blocks away across Peachtree Road. Nobody was hurt, and no houses went down, though a few trees did. The tornado was evidently hungry for mobile homes, found a park at the city's eastern fringe, and devoured that. (Does God despise mobile homes? Were they conceived in Original Sin?) It moved on eastward, we got our lights back as suddenly as they had vanished, and we looked at each other. Wordlessly, I got a book and a pillow and some candles and matches and went to the Killing Ground. Heyward and the two cats joined me. We sat there until sleep won over cowardice, and came back upstairs and went to bed.

The next three days were full of strange, abrupt winds that doubled back on themselves, green light, running cloud shadows, heavy, sudden stillnesses in which it was difficult to breathe. Something in the fabric of the air sent the cats mean and manic; tails would fatten and ears skin back and off they would go, sidewise, through the house and out the cat door, to return in a few minutes, walking low. We watched a great deal of television and had four distinct and senseless fights.

On Memorial Day proper, some alchemy had sucked the prickling danger from the air and it was an ordinary cloudy, warm May day. We went out to look at the damage in our yard. It wasn't as bad as the carnage the Big Ice had left, but it was a sizable

mess. And there were several monster trees, trees
that had always leaned protectively over our house,
that now leaned a little farther. And not nearly so
protectively. "Those have got to come down before
the next storm," Heyward said.

And so it was that the Brotherhood Tree Service
came into our lives.

In Atlanta, which is furred with cherished trees
like a slice of Sherwood Forest, tree services abound.
They range from the venerable, excellent, Establish-
ment Davey right down to pickup trucks whose
drivers leave cards in your mailbox saying "Fred's
Tree Service," or call you up and say they just happened to be driving past your place and noticed some
bad problems with the hickories, or whatever. We got
estimates from a representative sampling. I could
have had a very good time in Tiffany's for what
Davey was asking, and the pickup truck affairs
couldn't swear they could make it until about July
and looked to me to be manned by second-story men
to boot. Then a friend told us about the Brotherhood
Tree Service. Or at least he told us they were fast,
reliable, cheap, and bonded. We called. The price for
taking down four titans was absurdly low, but they
were bonded. . . .

Just as we were leaving for work on the appointed
morning, a psychedelically flowered Volkswagen bus
came lunging tipsily into our driveway, Sly and the
Family Stone bleating from the radio. Three young
men in Levi's tie-dyed to match the bus emerged.
They were bare from the waist up, with beads, peace
symbols, and the other amulets of the young bounc-
ing hollowly off their tender, downy young chests.
You could count three delicate sets of ribs with no

difficulty at all. All had truly beautiful, burnished, flowing hair to their shoulder blades, neatly tied at the nape with ribbons. They wore round gold wire-rimmed glasses in tints of yellow, mauve, and rose.

They were exceedingly polite and well-spoken young men, explaining sweetly that yes, it *was* an unusual name for a tree service, but that love and brotherhood should extend to all living things, trees especially, and that if you had to do such a bad thing as cut down a tree, well, you should have it cut by someone who loved it.

Feeling like materialistic tree murderers, we extracted their promise that the bloody deed would be accomplished by the time we returned and left, trying not to look at what was surely the original working model for all the chain saws in the world. "They're probably Druids or some damned thing," muttered Heyward, "and will come in our bedroom some night and drive a stake of ivy through our hearts."

"Holly," I corrected absently. "I thought they were nice kids." But we were very quiet on the drive into town.

When we rolled into our driveway that evening, the lawn looked like Pompei. Column-sized segments of trees were scattered over the yard, none of them of a size that we could, even together, budge an inch. The trees were down all right, down to neat, ground-level stumps. The Brotherhood Tree Service had been true to their word. But we still had the trees. Only in pieces.

"Did you ask them to take the trees away?" I said, smally. "Well, no," said Heyward, who was mottling suspiciously around the mouth. "But every other goddamn service I called said that was included in the price, so I just assumed . . ." We called. A fluting young feminine voice said she was sorry but the Brotherhood had decided trees weren't their thing any more, and had left that very evening to go and spread love and brotherhood among the migrant citrus pickers in Florida. "Mankind is their beat," breathed the nymphet as if by way of benediction. "They are beautiful, groovy people, and I will always love them." What Heyward said had none of love and benediction in it. The Brotherhood Tree Service had taken its revenge.

We began to call for someone to come and take the trees away. The earliest anyone could get to it was maybe in a week. Okay, we could live with it until then, though the price was comparable to a Harley-Davidson's. Except for one eight-foot section of trunk, about as thick in diameter as a Wagnerian soprano, which was protruding a little into the street, none of the debris directly impeded our living.

One typical late-to-work morning that week, when I had mindlessly dumped a five-pound bag of self-rising flour into the oven to put out the grease fire I had started with the bacon, cut myself shaving my legs, and run my last pair of runless pantyhose, the doorbell rang. Heyward had gone. It was a man from the sanitation department. "Lady," he said, "I'm sorry to be the one that has to tell you, but that tree you got sticking out in the road is on city property, and we gon' have to bring suit." Desperately, I launched into the saga of the Brotherhood. "Yes'm," he said, "we know about them guys. Got several suits pending right now because of them. Thing is, it don't matter *who* done the work, y'all are liable for the damage.

Course, if we could find 'em, we could get them, too."

"Forget it," I said bitterly, "unless you want to make a little trip to Florida. They're down comforting the migrant workers."

"Huh," he said. "I thought they was out in California with the grape pickers." At which point I burst into tears.

Getting, sobbing, into my car to go to work, I noticed that the jutting segment of errant tree had been placed neatly off the street and laid on our yard. Something in my tale of woe had touched the sanitation man. He and his fellow worker had saved us a suit and won themselves a lifelong ally.

I don't care how often they strike. I'll haul my own garbage for the rest of my life. And I hope the Brotherhood Tree Service gets, to a man, citrus acidosis.

The Coming of Crossroads

∞

I t was surely a celestial shove from my grandfather that brought Crossroads to us. In a late-spring twilight, Heyward and I were leaving a suburban shopping-center movie, threading through the rows of parked cars toward a small Italian restaurant we like, and I saw a cat crouched under our car. Or, rather, a vague, lumpy cat-shape with stabbing green eyes and the glint of a red collar. My husband saw it, too.

"No," he said. "Put it right out of your head. We are not going to Get Involved with Another Cat. Look, he has a collar on. He belongs to somebody. He's just waiting for somebody in the movie and resting in the shade. See how fat he is? I mean it, Anne. No."

"Cats don't sit under cars in shopping centers just for the hell of it," I quavered. "He's lost or abandoned. He's scared to death. He'll get run over if he even moves. Please, just let me . . ."

"*No.*"

119

I made it as far as the restaurant door before the tears got to chin level. "Oh, for God's sake," my husband said tiredly. "Come on. Let's go get the cat. But he's going to the Humane Society in the morning, and this time I'm not kidding."

I raced back to the car. "Here, kitty-kitty," I caroled in my best cat-fetching voice, expecting that we'd have to drag him, spitting and scratching, from under the car. A moment later, I had thirty-two pounds of purring tomcat in my arms.

He was startling to look at, and to this day I get a small, fresh shock when he comes rolling into a room. He is not a handsome cat. He is magnificently obese in the Charles Laughton manner. He has dainty feet and a truly unfortunate short, ropy, possumlike tail. His fur is a sort of rough Scotty brindle, so short and spiky that it separates into miniature, serrated Elizabethan ruffs around his short neck when he moves his cantaloupe-shaped head. The fur sits on thick, loose skin that you can move around, with the result that he looks like something in an ill-fitting cat suit, but we can't find the zipper. His face is pretty and poignant, like a Rouault clown. From behind, when he is trotting along on his short, bowed legs and little mincing feet, with his belly swinging, he looks like Babe Ruth trotting around the bases.

I was instantly in his thrall.

We put him into the back seat of the car and started home, but he would have none of that subordinate station. Before we were at the first traffic light, he was in my lap, roaring an anthem to companionship and salvation and kneading my stomach with his silly feet. This purr, which is audible two rooms away when he cranks up, sounds like an elderly blender stuck on high speed. He didn't meow for three months, and when he began to do so, it was a rusty, uncatlike sound that startled people. Asking for his dinner now, he still sounds like a century-old hinge.

We shut him into our bedroom to avoid the inevitable tantrum we knew would follow when he first met Peter and the Major. After nearly six years, they still loathed each other; we had no reason to think this hulking caricature of catdom was going to be welcomed with equanimity. After putting food, water, and kitty litter into the adjoining bathroom, we went out for our belated dinner. And we discussed a suitable name.

I have a theory that if you name a newly acquired animal, be he gift or derelict, right away, you have made him yours, and that only a heartless brute would wrest him away from you and take him to the Humane Society. My husband is not that, only cat-sated, and something in the clown-masked face must have gotten to him, because he entered into the naming program with considerable grace. I have, over the years, collected a few names that I consider especially appropriate for the sort of cats we get around here—huge, massive, and epically unadorable—and I trotted them out. "Wabash?" I ventured. "You know, as in 'Wabash Cannonball.' Chairman Meow? Rasputin?"

"Not right," said Heyward, regarding the depths of his martini as if the name lay there somewhere. "Try some more."

"Well, we've never used Piedmont. Palooka looks right, but . . . Cromwell, maybe. That weird round head. Bismarck? That head was just made for one of those iron helmets with the thing on top of it."

"No," said Heyward. "Crossroads. His name has got to be Crossroads, and I have no idea why."

So Crossroads he became, and my apologies to whoever owned him before we did, for someone did, surely. His astounding girth and rakish red leather collar and not-so-recent alteration spoke of doting and fussing, and I will always feel a trifle guilty that I never put an ad in the paper about him. I feel sure that some nice little old lady in a neat little apartment near that shopping center still calls, "Here, Tom," every night, and weeps into her lavender-scented pillow. Whoever you are, ma'am, there's a lady on Vermont Road who's taking fine care of your cat, and adores him, and you really should have been more careful.

We're fairly sure he's an apartment cat because he hates and fears the outdoors. He gets absolutely no exercise except the few daily ambushes he perpetuates on Peter and the Major—we were right; now we have *three* cats who hate each other—and has to be driven out into the fresh air at broom or shoe point. He will consent to waddle five feet away from the back steps to the rose garden, where the earth is soft, to relieve himself, but much prefers the plushy bath mat in the guest bathroom, which we keep closed at all times against his furtive onslaughts. But occasionally, we forget, and he hooks his steel-clawed paw around the door, opens it, streaks lumpishly inside, and achieves Karma. When we find the bath mat neatly folded over upon itself in a bundle, we know Crossroads has struck again.

His second favorite loo is the glass shower stall in our bathroom, and I have seen him hook open the door (which will never quite close), turn around, doglike, six or seven times, position himself directly over the drain, perform his rite, and then spend five minutes scrabbling peevishly at the tile. He knows somewhere in his pea brain, I suppose, that Cats Cover Their Waste. An enormous plastic litter box in the basement, kept fresh and deep and fragrant, has been ignored since his arrival. Where he did his thing at his former home I have no idea. Maybe I was wrong, and the little old lady flung him out into the shopping center in a fit of pique.

To add to his other dubious charms, he is not well. He has a Condition. Shortly after his arrival, his belly grew even more distended and awe-inspiring, and he took to moping upon pillows and drinking enormous amounts of water. I knew he was overweight, so I cut his rations to mere dabs. But he kept on ballooning, moaning, and belching. My husband crammed him into the cat carrier and took him to the vet, on what I was sure was a one-way trip. "He has a tumor," I wept, "and they're going to have to put him to sleep."

Heyward reports that when he opened the carrier and produced Crossroads our good and unflappable vet looked at him for a full second and said, in a tone of reverence, "Good God." I believe him. Guests who have never seen him often say the same thing. At any rate, Crossroads went in for observation and Heyward came home, where we awaited the verdict. That afternoon, the vet called.

"What is it?" I mewled, having answered the telephone.

"Well, Mrs. Siddons," said he, "he has a pancreatic condition that I believe we can control with four hundred units of vitamin E every day. It'll help him absorb his food. I've—uh—cleaned him out. But I'd say his main problem is that he's a neurotic, compulsive eater, and a sneak thief. He's been stealing food from somewhere."

He had, indeed—from the other cats, whom I was accustomed to feeding and leaving alone to dine in peace, since they both get spooked if pans and paper bags rattle. They were growing wan and querulous while Crossroads was eating himself to death. Now, I preside at the dinner hour whether they like it or not, wrap their dishes in foil and put them away when they're done, and generally spend more time trying to maintain balanced cat diets than I would if I had three infants. In addition, I dutifully smear an inch of a gelatinous, nasty substance coyly called Kit-Vite on my finger every evening and smear it on Crossroads's muzzle. It says on the Kit-Vite tube that the cat will love Kit-Vite and soon accept it right out of the container. Crossroads hates it and has to be anointed with it, so that he will lick it off his muzzle trying to rid himself of it, and so ingest it. A cat with a Condition is trying.

He has no idea he is not the most adorable and socially acceptable entity in Christendom, and attends every cocktail and dinner party we have ever had since his arrival, staying till the bitter end. Sometimes he favors a guest with his lap-stunning presence, but most often he sits on a gentleman's shoes. He has a shoe fetish that is not cute and has been, on more than one occasion, downright embarrassing. A charming and fastidious bachelor friend visited one week from Washington, a man whose *élan*, sophistication, and warmth is the joy of my heart, but who is not a natural lover of children and animals. He had not walked in the door before Crossroads had prostrated himself upon his highly polished shoes and performed an obscene, wriggling, rolling mime of love and admiration upon them. I don't know whether it was John or John's shoes that so besotted him, but he moved into John's room for the duration of his stay, and all attempts to oust him failed. When John was not in his shoes, Crossroads lay upon them, crooning in bliss. When they were on John's feet, he lay upon John's feet like a corrupt Buddha. It is a performance he repeats with some, but not all, of our male friends. Heyward thinks he has a penchant for Peale shoes. I think he is nuts, but then, what else, among the fauna at our house, is new?

He hates both Peter and the Major, but the gray Persian, who is a coward under his lionlike fluff, is his natural prey, and Crossroads lurks around corners and under chairs in order to feint at the Major's elegant behind whenever he floats past like a graceful gray clipper ship under full sail. Major Grey has learned to accept these sorties with an aloof and patently false dignity; you can tell that he wishes to kill Crossroads and will one day, if he can figure out a way to do it that doesn't involve bodily contact. Crossroads, however, contrived a new tactic of terror not so long ago that I truly do not think the Major will ever get over. I had left a large paper grocery bag lying in the middle of the kitchen floor, where it stayed for two or three hours before I got around to removing it. As I was going into the kitchen to do so, two things happened. The Major hove into view, rounding the door from the dining room into the kitchen. And the paper bag went scuttling crabwise across the floor straight at him. I shrieked, Crossroads's leering face appeared out of the bag, and the

Major left across the backyard for Chattanooga at forty miles an hour. Since then, Crossroads has moved into a paper bag we leave in the den for him, sleeping there all day until the Major puts a delicate, ruffed foot into the room, at which point the act is repeated. Crossroads never tires of it. And the Major never learns.

As I say, I have been in Crossroads's thrall since we first fished him out from under the car at the movie that spring evening. But enough is enough. Recently, a magnificently plumed, orange-eyed black Persian appeared in our back yard, howling for our three to come out and fight like men. Before I even examined his blooming neck for a collar, before I even glanced at his ribs for any evidence of malnutrition, I went to the back door and shouted, "Shoo!"

He was probably a shoplifter. I've got enough psychoses at my house.

SUMMER

Journey Through a
Distant Summer

One morning, almost precisely a week after the coming of Crossroads, I opened the back door into the green air and summer was there. Since I have been an adult, summer has been surprising me, sneaking up to my doorstep and just being there one morning. But it has not always been so.

When I was a child in Fairburn, Georgia—a small town then as it is now, but somehow bigger then—summer was not so much a time that came wheeling around in its own orderly, reassuring progression as it was a place you earned the right to inhabit for a while, after you had dutifully used up the rest of the year. Like a long, bright tunnel, it had an entrance, familiar landmarks, way stations, detours and side trips, a comfortable and readable terrain, and a clearly defined exit. And, like peach pie allowable only after you had finished your turnip greens, it was an award of merit. It was anticipated with pleasure, gobbled with haste, finished too soon, and rich enough to produce what, in my childhood, was called, flatly and graphically, "a little gas."

Summer put up its own road signs so you knew you were getting there. The first time you could go barefoot after school was one of them. Open schoolroom windows in long, dim, fly-buzzing afternoons, with the crack of bats from the athletic field to remind you that time never *would* pass, were another. Maypops were another—green, flower-starred spheres that you cut into baskets or carved faces on, like little emerald pumpkins—or, in prodigal abandon, squashed with your bare foot to hear the firecracker pop. Flourishing lava fields of kudzu were another. Like getting nearer to the beach after an interminable drive, you seized on each one with increasing, despairing elation. Open schoolroom windows were twenty miles. Barefoot was fifteen. Maypops—will we *ever* get there? How much farther?—were ten.

The door into summer was the last-day-of-school door, through which we spilled, shrieking and prancing, into June. "No more pencils, no more books, no more teachers' dirty looks!" Mothers, already damp with noon heat and promissory exasperation, warned us for the first of a thousand weary times not to let the screen door bang and made us tomato sandwiches for lunch.

June was a frenzy of things to do, devised either by us to exorcise the chalky, grieving ghosts of school or by our parents, to dissipate the awesome, fractious energy of pent-up little carnivores. It seemed that we could never use up June. June was playing Tarzan in the wonderful jungle of kudzu and honeysuckle behind my house, accepting the role of Cheetah with humble alacrity because the big boys up the street deigned to include me in exchange for the use of my kudzu. June was wearing a green garden snake in the pocket of your shirt—greener than all the green things in the world, with a hummingbird-flickering tongue that felt like a butterfly nibbling your arm— and producing it to scare your mother. June was getting too hot at noon and feeling a little sick from the powerful iced tea at lunch; swinging from the sternly forbidden vine off the dizzying heights of Indian Cave, your heart skidding high and sickly in your throat, but scareder of being a chicken than of being dead; stepping on your first bee. June was punching holes in the lids of Mason jars to house the fragile miracles of lightning bugs, who were always crushed in your efforts to be gentle, and left a chalky smear of moonlight on your fingers. June was the summer's first stomachache from illicitly copped plums, reaffirming the existence of a stern and righteous Creator. Hydrant water in cans, tasting of new tennis balls. The crusty, prehistoric carapaces of July flies stuck on the oak trees in my front yard. June was tying a string to the leg of a June bug, as exotic as an Egyptian scarab, and letting him bumble despairingly at the end of his tether till you lost interest or he lost his leg. June was crueler than the rest of the summer.

Two parent-planned projects clove into June, for the benefit of your soul and your mind, respectively. The first was Vacation Daily Bible School, where you spent every morning for two weeks, being prepared for productive future church service and learning Crafts. In the long, church-cool mornings, there was an alien, exotic quality to the stories of Ruth and Boaz, a catechistic mysticism to learning the names of all the books of the Bible. You trotted among the dim, brown-painted halls and small hot classrooms in sandals and shorts, feeling that, if your omnipresent parents sent you off clad that way to church, it must be okay with God, that He must declare a two-week moratorium on socks and starch every summer.

There were earnest, lip-chewing crafts sessions to break up the instruction. You produced ponderous papier-mâché ashtrays, drunken, tottering clay pots and pin trays, burned improbable things into wood, or sanded and shellacked obscure domestic wares, depending on your age and state of grace. You bleated with the baseball-field fervor of the young, "*Onward* Christian Sol-l-l-djurs, *marching* as to war-r-r" and "I will make you fishers-s-s-zov men." At recess under the trees in the churchyard, there was lemonade, milk, and the hands-down favorite strawberry Kool-Aid, with heat-faded banana and tuna fish sandwiches and animal crackers, potato salad that no citydweller could ever emulate, and vanilla ice cream, going plushy in Dixie cups before you could finish it. Recess was the province of a different squad of mothers every morning, who tried hard not to notice that their own offspring won the foot races or didn't win the Boy Scout flashlight awarded for faultlessly parroting the books of the Bible.

June was also the beginning of the summer reading program, held under the auspices of Fairburn's branch of the Carnegie Library. The library was in the Campbell County Courthouse, a huge old matron of a building, red brick and white-columned, built when our end of Fulton County was a separate county to itself, and court day brought a proper judge and droves of people into town in buckboards and Model-T

Fords. The Courthouse—for it has worn that name ever since its brief moment of judicial glory—inhabited its own square. Getting to the library was an ordeal by fire in the summer, for shoe-scorning pilgrims had a long stretch of searing pavement to cross before the cool tiles of the veranda assuaged the agony. From my house, it was a block-and-a-half trip—you started out at a jog and were running flat out in long leaps, like a gazelle, before you made it. Presumably, the soles of the faithful never bore the scars of the ordeal.

The library was the special domain of Miss Mamie Entrekin, a tall, gentle, white-haired maiden lady who had the sweetest smile and the greatest reverence for books I have ever had shed on me. The library smelled wonderful and was cool and silent, except for the twang-thud of the screened front door. Even if I hadn't been drawn to reading like a lemming to the sea, I would have liked to hang around in it. Miss Mamie let me work my way through the juvenile section into the hallowed adult division, sending me reeling and prancing home over the hot pavement under a chin-high stack of books every three or four days and never diverting my progress except to call my mother and alert her gently that I had checked out *Forever Amber* again. After the reading program began, the summer became one still, endless afternoon spent on the creaking glider on our screened side porch with, as my mother put it when trying to shoo me out from underfoot, "my nose stuck in a book."

In July, the real heat set in, and summer became a jellied, suspended thing. July meant spending days and weeks at my grandparents' farm, galumphing around in the miry creek at the bottom of the calf pasture, shooting the bored, tail-switching cows with slingshots made from old inner tubes, bickering and scuffling happily with my two cousins. July was loping, panting, rakehell dogs dripping moisture from their tongues, too enervated to bite the paper boy or the grocery boy or any of the winter's fair game. July was the ladies in my mother's missionary society in pretty cotton print dresses and talcum powder, fanning in the cool afternoon cave of our living room. July was paper fans from the funeral home moving in slow arcs in church on Sunday, the ghostly nighttime dissonance of katydids, the place in the summer where somebody dared you to eat poke berries, and you did and were very sick in the whispery, fever-floating big bed in your parents' room. Each July we made our ritual visit to St. Simons Island, and I felt strangely shy and tentative when I resumed my place in the small, strict ranks of my peers. It doesn't take long for a child to suffer a sea change. July was totally stopped and still, an underwater place.

In August, you began to see the end of the tunnel. Days were still blindingly hot, but there was a faint web of September on twilights and nights. Dew was chill and stinging on bare feet when you played kick the can after supper. Streets felt good after dark, still holding the heat of the day, and I would snuggle the length of me against my father's car, still sun-hot, while we told ghost stories, fighting off going in, going to bed, losing the night and the summer.

Late August was full of restlessnesses and rustlings, subterranean sighs and dyings and little pains. I remember one late August night, playing kick the can in the Segers' back yard, with bugs committing small, ticking suicides against the street lights and winter crouching off at the edge of the dark. I ran through a rosebush and gained a long, deep scratch on my thigh. I still have the scar.

I don't remember the pain now, but the scar of August is still on me. I only regret that it hurts a little less every year.

Reunion in Princeton

We came to Princeton, New Jersey, on a stifling Tuesday last June, in a racketing, ill-tempered rental car picked up in Philadelphia. It was three o'clock in the afternoon when we drove in through the postcard-pretty truck farms and fields that surround the town, in past Palmer Stadium ("Oh, Heyward, even the stadium has ivy on it!") and the old brick and stone houses that once housed who knows what affluent tradesmen and faculty members, and now house near-identical swarms of barefoot, Levi'ed students, some of whom are women.

They were sitting on stone walls and verandas, stripped as far as decency allowed against the smothering New Jersey heat, watching the rental cars and station wagons full of wilted alumni and families stream in for Reunion Week. It was my husband's twenty-fifth—Class of '48, the Big One, as the pennants and orange beer cans, courtesy Budweiser,

136

under the great tent in the quadrangle that served '48 as its headquarters, proclaimed. He hadn't been back since the middle fifties, and those tall, grave young colts with long sheens of smooth hair were the first women undergraduates he had ever seen on the Princeton campus.

"Goddammit, it just doesn't look right," he growled, and I giggled. I had come to Princeton primarily to giggle. Indeed, I had been giggling ever since the previous November, when a letter arrived for me which began, "Dear '48 Wife: Well, the Big One is coming up. And here's a chance to really please your old man this Christmas. For only $49.95, you can order his class blazer in time for . . ."

A product of the rural South and graduate of a large southern university whose lackadaisical alumni can hardly be persuaded to attend anything but boozy, murderous football weekends where they wear orange felt beanies and howl obscenities at Bear Bryant, I simply knew nothing about the graceful ritual of the Ivy League reunion. In fact, the very thought of middle-aged men in beer jackets, wailing "Going Back to Old Nassau" on the gray stone steps of that august edifice and pounding each other on the back while examining each other covertly for signs of encroaching senility, struck me as one of the funniest things I'd ever envisioned. And when the schedule of events for Reunion Week duly arrived, I read it and did a great deal of grousing. "You get to do all kinds of neat things like going to stag smokers and class dinners and being in the P-rade—whatever the hell that is," I whined. "And I get to tour the president's rose garden with a bunch of wives who all went to Smith or somewhere and doubtless belong to the

Merry Giggle Hunt and play tennis together and will have on some little Valentino nothing and think I'm a hick."

In regrettable point of fact, I have always been a bit in awe of Heyward's glossily ivied classmates and their Tasteful backgrounds, and have envied those who walked easily in the cloistered world of Princeton and its peers ever since I read Scott Fitzgerald (who apparently never stopped carrying a big stick while he walked there softly, either). I have the traditional insular, truculent Southerner's distrust of the East and would dearly love to be able to toss off references to tea at Dean Conant's, or the Yale-Princeton weekend when we went back to Colonial and ran into old Thornby, who's just back from the Middle East and tells such marvelous stories about Faisal.

But I can't, and no husbandly attempts to assure me I would Fit Right In and Everybody would Love Me assuaged the niggling certainty that the men would tease me kindly like a retarded child and the women would tell me what a sweet dress I had on, and everybody would agree behind our backs that old Siddons certainly had himself a quaint little second wife.

So I took refuge in ridicule and managed to make quite an ass of myself to our friends in Atlanta before we left.

On that Tuesday afternoon, though, I was a little subdued. We had made a short detour earlier in order to drive through the campus of the Lawrenceville School, and I had fallen under the spell of those great, dreaming old brick buildings and mammoth elms and green playing fields where Dink Stover and the Tennessee Shad had earned themselves immortality and a place in my heart long ago, when I read Owen Johnson's wonderful *Lawrenceville Stories*. They had seemed as remote and underwater to me then as *The Wind in the Willows* and *The Secret Garden*, pure, gentle fantasy. But there was the Jigger Shop, and there the football field where Dink underwent his first rite of passage, and there the infamous dormitory roof. Something began to curl into my head like old, old smoke.

We nosed into a parking space and got out, pulling sticky clothes away from our backs. "It's early yet to go out to Kiki's," said Heyward. "Let's cut through the main gate, and I'll buy you a drink at the Nassau Tavern." We walked in the hot, timeless afternoon, under vaulting old elms and cedars, past gray stone buildings with Gothic arches and leaded windows. There was an odd quiet, as old and deep as an ocean.

Through it we could hear a muffled splashing, and between two clumps of ancient cedars we had a long vista down to a small, heat-mirrored lake. A long, graceful shell was fleeing over its surface, with a lean, synchronized crew pulling effortless oars. The lead man had a megaphone. "Are they . . . ?"

"Sculling," said Heyward, looking sidewise at the silly little smile curving my mouth.

A bell with a voice like eternity spoke four times, lost somewhere up in the canopy of green, its notes hanging long and bronze and perfect in the ringing air. A young professor with a fine beard was gesturing to a handful of students slouching on the grass under an enormous elm across the campus. "It's all a stage set," I said, but I said it sleepily, sliding into the day and the place. The Princetonization of Annie had begun.

Princeton's Reunion Week, I learned during its course, is probably the most ceremonial and time-hallowed in the Ivy League. All the classes that have living members attend, from '03 up to the newly graduated class. Each has its own headquarters, usually under a canopy in one of the school's countless gray-bastioned quadrangles, and these enclaves are as distinct in ethos and as jealously guarded as an Englishman's club in the savage tropics. Each class has its own uniform, and they range from a perfunctory orange fedora and black-patterned tiger tie (Class of '25, I think) to the full and correct regalia of the Class of '48: gray slacks, white shirt, orange-and-white striped seersucker blazer, tiger-patterned tie, white bucks, and white straw boater with orange band. Some later classes, with only a few attending, were sensible in Bermuda shorts and T-shirts. Some space-age alumni sweltered in silver nylon space suits. One class pu.ddled around in swathing Batman capes. There were maybe fifteen hundred alumni on campus, all dressed in whatever their class had espoused for the week, and the result was absurdly like Disney World, moved lock, stock, and barrel into the Cathedral of Notre Dame. Perhaps even more absurdly, it didn't look absurd. Princeton Reunion Week, like *The Turn of the Screw*, has the ability to suspend one's belief in an orderly, rational universe.

The twenty-fifth reunion, no matter what the individual class, is always the *pièce de résistance* and the best attended, and when we drifted up to the gate of Heyward's, where a genial, sweating guard admitted us, the scene beyond looked like a marriage of a garden party to a scene from *The Greatest Show on Earth*. A canopy covered the entire quadrangle, which had been deeply sawdusted. Long, wooden trestle tables were full of orange men and summer-frocked women drinking complimentary Budweiser served up from a long bar by amiable, only slightly supercilious undergraduates. At another long table, pretty coeds dispensed reunion kits, T-shirts, boaters, pennants, and the indispensable badges shouting CLASS OF '48 and your name, without which you hadn't a prayer of getting into any of '48's activities. A rock band was booming, throngs of children were shrieking underfoot, clumps of balloons bloomed in corners, assorted campus dogs lolled in the cool, damp splotches where the beer coolers leaked. Virtually all the men, being identically clad, looked like my husband, everybody seemed to know everybody but us, it was precisely 100 degrees under the Big Top, and I had a desperate urge to run and take refuge in a dark, air-conditioned movie theater. Or even better, a bar. Taking a deep breath, we dove into Reunion.

It was a week to be remembered as you might remember a dreamlike snorkel under the waters of the Great Barrier Reef. The regular, slow turning of each sun-stricken day was punctuated by ritual: breakfast in the cool, dim Commons or the air-conditioned haven of the Nassau Tavern. Tennis or a father-son softball game down on the burning field. The eleven o'clock beer, tepid before you finished it, under the tent, where Heyward's classmates proved to be genuinely nice and did remember him fondly and did not patronize me, although some few were indeed in the diplomatic corps or the Cabinet, and one was Bowie Kuhn. I learned to my reassurance that even Cabinet members go gray or balding, that even captains of industry have shy second wives, that even Bowie Kuhn sweats under a stifling canopy and removes his limp jacket. I learned that even heiresses get limp-haired and grass-stained at 100 degrees and chase children just as peevishly as my own friends and, moreover, did not patronize me, being unsure that a sweating, grass-stained, anonymous southern wife was not one of them. Sweat is a great leveler.

Lunch, if you hadn't fled again to the Nassau Tavern, was fried chicken and hot dogs and potato salad and beer, and there were regularly scheduled afternoon tours of the museum, or erudite lectures on "Agribusiness in the Electronics Age" and "The Future of the Humanities in the Coming Technocracy," but I think everybody went back to his hotel or motel room and slept. We crept back, each afternoon, to the lovely two-hundred-and-some-year-old farmhouse out in nearby Hopewell, where an exceedingly forbearing friend of my husband's family gave us a week's openhearted hospitality, and fell into heat- and beer-stunned sleep, cool at last within two-foot-thick stone walls.

All over the campus and out in the beautiful old town, in the evenings, there were cocktail parties, where refreshed alumni and wives gathered for cool drinks and civilized talk. Ostensibly. At the first one, scrubbed and resplendent in long, crisp white piqué, and hollow from a day of sweating and no food, I got gently and sweetly drunk on two gin and tonics, lost my identification badge and earrings, called a something-or-other of Protocol in Washington a pussycat, jitterbugged baroquely with the publisher of some impeccable little literary quarterly, and fell asleep propped against the host's Silver Cloud, talking to an elegant lady about Molière—a gentleman about whom I know nothing at all. I was wakened and taken home in disgrace by my properly mortified husband, and cringed redly into the wee hours at the thought of encountering the Protocol Man, the Publisher, or the Elegant Lady the next day. As it turned out, none of them remembered any of it. It was that kind of week.

But it was another kind of week, too, one that touched a deep chord within me, a well of poignance and simple love of continuity and tradition that, having no special academic traditions of my own to draw from, I never knew I had. Already bemused by the long heat, the very tangible old spell of the university, and the strong undercurrent of nostalgia running through the week, I understood on the last Saturday at least a part of what draws these men, brisk, productive, good grown men, back like children to a picnic every year.

It was the Saturday of the P-rade, the one event which had amused me most of all on the activities list. "Dear heaven, Heyward, fifteen hundred grown men all dressed up and marching? From where to where? It sounds like the Elks." And my husband had grinned uncertainly, because he'd never been to a P-rade either. For that uncertain grin, for that diminishment of pleasure, however slight, I have ached and repented since last June.

On the morning of the P-rade, under the tent, something slightly scalp-crawling was building up.

We wives clung closer together, in tight knots, feeling our men draw away from us at last and into the body of '48, into a whole where we couldn't follow, as if into the ranks of Eleusinian initiates. Into Princeton. The Class Picture was taken on the steps of Blair Arch, and we saw them all together for the first time, a tiered shoal of orange and black and pride. The rock band, which had for days been whumping out Bacharach and Jim Croce, crashed into "Going Back to Old Nassau," and I heard it for the first time, this song I had giggled so gleefully at, rolling at me across Princeton University as it had, on this same day, for reunions out of mind. I couldn't find my husband in the throng and wouldn't have known him if I had; they were all gone away from us now. I couldn't see through the lens of my borrowed Nikon for the tears, but there were two hundred and fifty '48 wives who were fogging up their lenses, too, so it didn't matter.

After the picture was taken, women in quiet groups moved away across campus to find seats along the P-rade route. It ran about a mile and a half, from Nassau Hall and the main gate down to the athletic field. The elm-shaded streets were literally jammed: with the wives and families of fifteen hundred alumni, with faculty and student body, with townspeople ranging from elderly, erect old men to young mothers in Bermuda shorts and groggy babies in strollers. Along with a sturdy, brisk girl who had been to several reunions and, therefore, knew the ropes and the best viewing spots, I found a niche on the curb in front of my husband's club. For what seemed a very long time, while the classes massed in their prescribed ranks back at the main gate, we waited; it was a pleasant crowd, but a quiet one.

And then you heard it, very faint, very far away, the percussion first: "Goin' back . . . goin' back . . . goin' back to Nassau Hall . . ." and then a regular cadence, which turned out to be the feet of marching men, and then fifteen hundred male voices, aged twenty-one to ninety-one, ". . . goin' back . . . goin' back . . ."

And then the band turned the corner, the sound rolled down the old street like a tidal wave, and, "Oh, God," I sobbed to brisk, no-nonsense little Ginny, who'd been through this so many times and was surely going to laugh at me, "I'm going to make the most awful damned fool of myself." But her face was buried in her hands and her shoulders were shaking, and she didn't hear me.

They were absolutely beautiful, these Princeton men marching by on a sunny June Saturday, and I don't give a holy hoot in hell that I cried for the one hour and fifteen minutes it took them to pass me. The band; then the tall, new young president, smiling; then, in the place of honor directly behind him, the Class of '48. Row after orange row of them, singing their song on their day on their street on their campus. I couldn't spot Heyward, but I'm glad; he told me later they'd all been trying hard not to weep openly, and nobody would look at his wife.

Behind them came perhaps the most poignant and gallant of them all, the Old Guard: the very oldest living Princetonians, singing "Going back . . ." for what surely must have been, for some of them, the last time. We had seen them during the week, in the Tavern or ambling about campus, natty in their bright uniforms, but so frail, so tentative, some leaning on menservants, some with gentle, bewildered old wives on their arms. Some of them will never make that march, I'd thought, not in this heat. And indeed, some were waving jauntily to the crowd from an open limousine. But others, by God, walked every step of the way, swinging along erect and vibrant, with perhaps only the common cord of Princeton sustaining them. And one, Class of '15, rode a unicycle. Roars of pure love swelled to meet them; there were many children and grandchildren and even great-grandchildren in the crowd, and more than one had a son and grandson marching with them, in other classes. But had there been no kindred soul there for any of them, they would have affected us the same. As they turned the corner onto Prospect Street, the crowd rose spontaneously to its feet, sun hats off, and all along the street they rose till the entire street was lined with standing people as the Old Guard went marching by.

And so it went, class after class, getting younger and brisker of step, until the seniors ended it up, the largest of all, starred with young girls' faces, singing, "Goin' back . . . goin' back."

Trudging back to headquarters, steaming hot and sunburned and emptied of emotion, I got lost and had ample time, wandering through the maze of shady quadrangles, to ponder why this simple, almost simplistic ritual, this near-archaic tribal rite, had moved me so deeply. I came to no conclusions. It seemed to me then, lost on that campus itself lost to time, that it was simply a right and good thing to honor something you loved very much as loudly and wholeheartedly as you could, and the devil take sophistication, civilization, undue examination, or whatever else threatened to get between you and it.

"Have you been crying?" said Heyward, when I finally found him under the canopy.

"Shut up," I said, "and get me a beer."

I Don't Like New York in June

On a day while we were in Princeton last June, before Reunion Week geared up, my husband and I went into New York for a flying visit. And wished we hadn't.

It had been precisely ten years since I had been to New York, but before that I'd visited often, staying with assorted city-struck friends in their impossibly cramped, cluttered, and overpriced cubbyholes in the East Eighties, sleeping on sofas and Hide-a-Beds and loving every hectic minute of it. It was the dream of all of us, stuck like yearning, iridescent flies in the amber of our Alabama college, to Go to New York when we graduated, but only a few of us did. In the late fifties, in the South, the distance to New York was measured in more than miles.

The New York to which we aspired never existed. It couldn't have. Nothing in it was real, and no subsequent visits ever breathed gritty, grimy life into it for

those of us who didn't live there. It was a scale model
built by Stanford White and Le Corbusier, threaded
by shining streets from the MGM back lot. The people who lived in its Billy Baldwin-appointed apartments and worked in its Knoll-furnished offices
(always advertising agencies and publishing houses)
were Piper Laurie and Millie Perkins and Tony Fran-
ciosa and Cary Grant, if you needed an Older Man, or
else Rona Jaffe had invented them. *The Best of Everything* was our field manual. Gordon Jenkins wrote the
score.

I visited often enough then, in those pre-riot-and-
rape days, to learn my way around the parts of New
York that mattered to anyone I cared to know. The
Eighties, where five underpaid sorority sisters who
did not, after all, have Careers but only toiled as secretaries to underwriters, lived what had to be the
Good Life in a one-bedroom apartment. There, in
that badly painted, ostentatiously doormanned
Xanadu, bullfight posters stood in for Billy Baldwin,
but the address was good.

Central Park—the part with high curly bridges that
was invariably photographed with Audrey Hepburn
in blue jeans running through it. Park-Fifth-Madison.
The theater district, vaguely. The prescribed lap
around the prescribed museums. One small area
around Gramercy Park (I adored knowing you had to
have a key to get into the park). I could eventually
find my way to the Village, had been taken to Sutton
Place, was fond of saying that Mary McCarthy made
Tudor City fashionable with *The Group*, and was
proud of myself for having ventured as far west as
Columbus Circle to prowl through the Huntington
Hartford.

It didn't occur to me that real people lived anywhere but my territorial Manhattan. I wouldn't have been interested in anybody who lived in the other four boroughs, didn't know about Long Island, sneered at the suburbs, and left midtown only once, when I took the wrong train and ended up somewhere near Carnarsie. To me, Brooklyn had a tree and a bridge.

But my ersatz Manhattan *was* a lovely place to visit, and so my memories of it were cherished, if celluloid: Watching the entire mounted patrol coming home two by two under the mist-haloed street lights one October evening. Flocks of birds—starling, I suppose—darting in luminous clouds around the top of the Empire State Building on a martini-enchanted June night. Standing in an April rain on the sidewalk outside McSorley's while my date had a beer inside, clutching his propitiary bunch of violets in white-gloved hands and finding nothing at all degrading about it. Talking to a man who turned out to be Robert Morse in P. J. Clarke's, drinking green beer in Costello's on St. Patrick's Day, having champagne with a peach in it at the Plaza (*Saratoga Trunk*-inspired champagne, canned peach). Dashing into Tiffany's as it closed in a new tweed suit from Bergdorf's to "pick up a little something for my hostess" (key ring). For years, I turned into Holly Golightly whenever my plane touched down at La Guardia.

Well knowing what usually happens to one's youthful Shangri-las when they are revisited, I should have been prepared. I should have suspected something when we learned that the ageless train that has always run from Princeton Junction to Penn Station—the one my husband remembers from his idyllic college years—didn't any more, with any regularity. Many people took the bus now, we were told, and it was only a nice, cool hour's ride straight into the New York Port Authority Terminal, where there was always a line of waiting cabs. So we dutifully bought our tickets on the nine-thirty bus to New York and went across the street to the bench in front of the main gate that is the bus stop to wait. It was nine-fifteen and we had a lunch date on Park. Plenty of time. No sweat.

Figuratively, anyway. At nine-fifteen in Princeton it was 92 degrees under a tree. I was dressed in what people who lunched on Park wore in my days there— little sleeveless linen dress, stockings, pumps. By the time the wayward bus coughed up to its stop at ten twenty-five, my pantyhose felt like a wet suit and my linen looked like used aluminum foil on a thawing chicken. We climbed aboard.

The bus windows were properly sealed to facilitate the air-conditioning that wasn't working. The driver was angry at having to stop for us and got angrier at each subsequent stop. They are legion between Princeton and New York. All in towns that looked as though they had factories and mills that were at that moment violating the child labor laws. The towns of the Jersey flats are to me the saddest and seediest places I have ever seen, and the hottest. People who got on at the last stops along the route had to stand, and the lady who was standing next to my seat was sucking Certs, listening to a transistor playing "Honey," and poking my chin with a large, round plastic hatbox-thing that had a Caesar's Palace sticker on it. When I wriggled one foot out of its blue-and-

white spectator pump, sweat had stained my foot
blue. When I half rose to unwrinkle my linen behind,
my sweat-slackened stocking foot slid around so that
I had a blue ring around one entire ankle. It wasn't
shaping up into any Gordon Jenkins day in New
York.

Finally, we were disgorged into the maw of the
Port Authority Terminal, which is as fearsome a place
as I hope to encounter while living. A catacombs-like
terminal area was spilling a lava of suburban types
onto concrete aprons—nice little hatted ladies who'd
brought their own E. J. Korvette shopping bags;
vaguely middle-aged men in electric blue double-
knits; young women in four-inch clogs and the varnished beehives and miniskirts of the late sixties; cool
young black men in what I can only describe as pimp
suits, with hard, measuring eyes; wiry young black
women with the high, rolling gaits of Shetland
ponies; one or two chic matrons with distaste ironed
onto their faces; Heyward and me. The herd made for
the terminal proper, where an arctic gust of public-
smelling air-conditioning froze our steaming clothes
to us in permanent ridges. Elbowed, jostled, and
glared at in impersonal malice on all sides, I began to
flinch.

This was no twilight-in-front-of-St.-Patrick's
crowd. A young Puerto Rican was performing an
eerie, slow-motion dance in a semicircle in front of
a phone booth where no phone was, chanting to
himself in high, sibilant island Spanish; his eyes
were half-lidded and opaque, and he was smiling at
his lost inner visions. An old man was slumped
against a Keys-Made-While-U-Wait booth, asleep or
drunk or ill or dead. He had soiled his pants. The

keymaker was making keys and people were stepping over him and a cop down the arcade looked
through him.

"Should we . . . ?"

"No."

Outside, where the taxi line waited, Port Authority
veterans body-checked us away from cab after cab. In
the last one, a driver with a tight, furious face fanned
himself with a tabloid and listened to a talk show.
Desperately knocking aside a small lady and her
sullen teenaged daughter, we lunged at it, ripped
open the door, scrambled in, and panted, "Park and
Forty-seventh. Please."

"Whassamattercan'tyoureadthemuthuhfuckingoff-
dutysign?"

"It's not on," said Heyward, getting the flat, polite
look on his face that means he's going to do battle
even though he be slain for it.

I thought he probably was, and mewled smarmily,
"Oh, that's all right. We'll just wait for—"

"YOUR OFF-DUTY SIGN IS NOT ON AND WE WANT TO GO
TO PARK AND FORTY-SEVENTH!" roared my husband.

"Muthuhfuckingsonofabitch," commented the
driver, and clashed into gear and careened off across
town.

It was after noon, and the traffic was hideous. The
cab was plastered with stickers that read AMERICA—
LOVE IT OR LEAVE IT and NIXON NOW, more than ever.
The plastic shield, designed, no doubt, to protect our
driver's tender sensibilities from the dangerous, left-
ist likes of us, was opaque with grime, and the driver's neck had a carbuncle. He cursed monotonously
and matter-of-factly and steadily, breaking his litany
of choler only to shout perfunctory obscenities at

other motorists, blow his horn, and thump on the side of his vehicle. I didn't really blame him. Every panel truck in Manhattan was double-parked along our route across town, effectively blocking any progress.

Approaching midtown, a shining cliff of a Lincoln just in front of us rammed the cab in front of it. Everything stopped. Horns started. The Lincoln's driver, a tanned, gray-frosted man in a silk suit got out and approached the other cab's driver, who was rolling down his window and turning a deep, dull red. The silk-suit man was an extra from *my* Manhattan; he looked like the Rector of Justin, and I was relieved to see that his type still existed. He looked into the cab's window and said in a satisfying bass Yale drawl, "I believe you were at fault."

"Go fuck yourself," said the cab's driver, uncoiling from his vehicle.

"Move that fucking thing!" roared our driver helpfully, leaning on his horn.

"I'll report you to the Hack Bureau," said the Rector of Justin, backing off slightly from his outraged adversary.

"I'll take you apart," said his driver, squaring off to do so.

"Go fuck yourself," the Rector of Justin said, and got back into his Lincoln and locked the door.

"Fuck you," said the cabbie, and got back into his cab and growled away.

"Fuck everybody!" shouted our driver creatively, and he blew his horn, and we were off again.

"If everybody in New York did that when somebody told them to, it would look like something

Bosch painted," I told Heyward, reeling from the exchange. When we crawled out on our corner and Heyward tipped our driver, I think he advised us to perform the same anatomical impossibility upon ourselves.

We ran into Saks to pick up a gift for our hostess in Princeton. Saks is—or used to be—a great font of civility and comfort to me, and I approached the inevitable black-dressed, duchess-faced chatelaine of the department with relief and alacrity.

"I'm looking for something for a country patio—an Italian cachepot or a pottery box or something," I said, "for around fifteen dollars. I'd like it in green and—"

"Pottery is in another department," snapped the Eighteenth Duchess of Saks. "All this is Limoges. I have to go to lunch now." And she did.

"Mmf-you," said my husband to her retreating ramrod back. And we left and walked across the street to keep our lunch date.

We were lunching with an old friend, a prep-school classmate of my husband's who is a long-time Manhattanite. He had visited us often in Atlanta, but we'd never called on him on his native turf. As he steered us out on Park into the lunchtime throng, he suffered a sea change into something rich and strange indeed. The amiable, graceful, urbane Charles I knew became a feral battering ram, cutting through the clotted crowd like a cruising shark. He towed me along behind him with a steel hand on my arm. "For Chrissake, how long has it been since you've been to New York?" he barked at me. "Only a damned fool would bring a handbag into the city. Every woman over twelve carries her money in her underwear, if she wears any. Give me that thing." And this shining six-foot son of St. Albans and Harvard went bruising down Forty-seventh Street clutching my dainty patent envelope to his chest and enjoining pedestrians he jostled to fuck themselves.

"New York is a summer festival," I quavered at him, hoping to inject a note of levity into the Bataan-like march to lunch.

"New York is a goddamn muggers' convention and don't you forget it," he flared.

At lunch, the Charles I knew was back, lighting my cigarettes and nodding affably to his publishing peers and trading courtesies with the headwaiter, who fell on his neck the instant we entered and installed us at an impeccable banquette that did not, for the first time on one of my New York visits, back up to the kitchen. He crooned over us and suggested the ubiquitous striped sea bass that all of New York seems to lunch on. I had three Bloody Marys in rapid succession and felt better.

Lunch over, we trudged back to Charles's office on Park, dropped him off, and stood for a moment on a corner, sniffing the wind. Things were looking up. I had borrowed the key to the ladies' room from Charles's enameled secretary and washed my face and hands, scrubbed most of the manacle-like ring of blue shoe dye off my ankle, squirted on a reviving splash of Vent Vert, and combed my hair. At three o'clock, the shadows of encircling buildings had cooled Park a little, and the crowds had thinned down to good-looking women whisking out of stores and restaurants and good-looking men getting out of cabs with attaché cases. Only an occasional young, lounging, sleepy-faced felon had ventured, barracuda-like, out of his territory to stalk his prey. This was more like *my* Manhattan.

"Want to stay in town and see a show?" asked Heyward, basking in the sunlit edge of the jungle. And at that moment, we witnessed our first purse-snatching.

I'm sure it wasn't much of a purse-snatching, as such things go: a rapier-quick sortie by a blind-faced child—he couldn't have been more than twelve—at a woman coming out of Saks's revolving door across the street, up to her eyes in muted, tweed-patterned Saks boxes. He had her shoulder bag and was around the corner and gone before her boxes hit the sidewalk and her mouth opened. She never did scream. "Somebody just took my purse," she said to people passing on the sidewalk, in a funny, small Connecticut voice. "I just had my purse snatched." Nobody broke stride, but one man did turn to look at her. She picked up her boxes and went back into the cool, dark maw of Saks.

"Did you see that?" asked Heyward, mildly.

"Yes," I said. "I want to go back to Princeton." And we did.

Coming back on the plane to Atlanta after Reunion Week, I told my husband about my Manhattan, and the things I remembered, and how New York had gone unalterably and certainly to hell, and how I would probably never go back. "Atlanta has its problems," I said prissily, "but the whole *city* isn't a damned jungle. People don't curse you as a matter of course. People don't try to *kill* you at lunchtime."

We claimed our baggage, staggered with it out of

the terminal, and lunged for the door of the last cab parked in the hack line under the canopy.

"Whassamatter," said the driver, "can'tyouread-themuthuhfuckingoffdutysign?"

A Southern Ghost Is Not
Your Ordinary Haunt

Reeling queasily out of a Sunday matinee of *The Exorcist* last summer, I told my husband and the couple we were with that such a bestial diabolical possession could not have happened in the Deep South. Not, at least, in the Deep South of my childhood.

"Why?" asked our friend David, who is an author and loves to dissect my sloppy, ambiguous pronouncements until he has forced me to consider what I really want to say. "Were the people in your South too sanctified for a demon to get ahold of? Or too shiftless and no-account for a self-respecting demon to mess with?"

"There weren't anything but Baptists and Methodists in Fairburn when I was growing up," I told him. "And I can't imagine a demon taking up with either one. Catholics or atheists, maybe, but not a Southern Baptist or Methodist."

We had coffee at a deli near the theater and pur-

sued the subject. Pinned to the wall, I finally decided
that what I'd meant was that Southern ghosts, ghouls,
shades, apparitions, demons, and other manifestations are less alien than the supernatural fauna and
flora of other regions. More at home with people. Or
at least, Deep Southerners seem to live more easily
with them.

When I was a child in Fairburn, there were several
well-established local haunts. Most were the sole
property of the little world. They faded at puberty
along with mustard plasters for chest colds and
galoshes and leggings. The adults in our lives gave
them short shrift, but they were as familiar to us as
the town eccentrics, the phallus-like monument to
our World War I dead that rose in the center of town,
and Dr. Amoss's drugstore. We didn't invent them;
somehow, when you reached a certain age and state
of credibility, you were told about them by the older
kids. I think they were kept alive by generations of
Fairburn children.

One was the Dog. The Dog was one of our most
ubiquitous haunts. You'd see him anywhere, at any
time between twilight and daybreak. He was various-
ly described by the kids who claimed to have seen
him as a huge, mastiff-like creature, a white, fleeting
collie, a skulking, silent, emaciated yellow animal, or
a black wolf-like creature who followed just behind
you on soundless feet. There was general agreement
on only two points: You could see through him, and
he didn't seem to exist for any purpose. His coming
wasn't the especial harbinger of death, ill luck, or
even a change in the weather.

In light of his innate innocuousness, I don't know
why the Dog scared us all witless, but he did. Far

more than the Cold Spot under the railroad under-
pass (if you stepped in it, you'd be dead within the
year), or the Light that flickered bluely on a certain
tombstone in the old cemetery at the edge of town (if
it moved from the tombstone and began to follow
you, you'd be dead within the year). Maybe it was
because those two latter manifestations, while deadly
and terrible, were fixed stars in our small firmament;
you could leap over the Cold Spot and forgo passing
the cemetery at night. But the Dog was apt to pop up
anywhere.

Most Dog sightings occurred near the log structure
next to the red brick jailhouse, which has been called
the Scout Hut ever since I can remember. The Cub
Scouts and Boy Scouts met there every Wednesday
night, and it was sacrosanct to Fairburn's young male
elite. The Dog was fond of appearing out of the stone
foundation of the Scout Hut and silently accompanying late-lingering Cubs to their homes, one pace
behind them, vanishing only when the yellow porch
lights of home dissolved him like a salted snail. But
he'd been seen other places, too. He escorted several
children home from forbidden autumn twilight forays
to the shuffleboard court on the school grounds to
roller skate. He used to walk J. L. Moss home from
his late paper route once a week. And there was a certain shallow place in the swift-running creek out at
Indian Cave that he frequented at summer sundowns;
the story in that instance was that he couldn't cross
water, so you were safe and could chunk rocks and
clods at him with impunity. These, of course, passed
through him like a BB through ground fog.

Because of his penchant for the Scout Hut and its
proximity to the jail, one or two halfhearted theories

sprang up about the Dog's origin: that he died outside the jail pining for his master, a murderer who was hanged there; that he was the spirit of a black conjurer who died in a cell swearing to put a conjure on the whole town. But even the smallest of us knew viscerally that Fairburn had never had a murder or hanged anybody, and the blacks we knew who were said to have Power were gentle people who worked in the yards and kitchens of our homes and wouldn't have harmed a hair of our heads. So the theories died.

But the Dog stayed until we reached age twelve or so, when he became invisible to us and appeared in turn to a new rank of cadets. I've often wondered where we got him. Not one of us had ever heard of lycanthropy; the only skin-turners we knew of were played by Lon Chaney on the patched screen of the decrepit movie house, and water never stopped him. I have later read of the phantom dog who runs like a thread through a thousand years of English and Scottish history, in various forms; I believe he's been called Black Sutch, the Black Dog, the One of the Four Legs, and other things and was probably a working model for *The Hound of the Baskervilles*. But we could not have known that then. I think, rather, that Fairburn, being settled over two hundred years ago by immigrant Scots who came down from the Southern Appalachian Highlands, had its own version of a thousand-year-old tale going. To me, that's a nice thought. I rather think, too, that the Dog—and I only half disbelieve in him to this day— was merely looking out for the only ones who gave him credence and being: the children. He knew when we didn't need him anymore. And he knew who did.

Aside from the Dog, whom we had in common, most Fairburn children had a household haunt or two all their own. These came to us from the black women who were our mothers' maids, who stayed with us in the long, light summer twilights or the early black winter evenings, when our parents were playing bridge up the street or attending a church function. These haunts were not given us to frighten us into obedience; a callused black hand on our backsides accomplished that far better than a ghost. They were shared with us, passed solemnly and matter-of-factly from vision-haunted black minds to the simple children's minds that were the only ones capable of receiving them without laughter. The world of haunts and hauntings was a secret bond between the white children and the blacks of Fairburn.

This was a world where doors were painted blue against evil spirits; pure Dahomean voodoo and a thousand years old, I know now. I still see blue-painted doors on Gullah shacks on the Sea Islands of Georgia and South Carolina. But then they were uniquely Fairburn's.

It was a world where "guppies" would drop from low-hanging tree branches onto your back and ride you in the night until you crawled home to die of exhaustion in bed. A caul from a newborn calf in your pocket would thwart a guppy, and a nail bent into a knot would, too. Were the "guppies" of my childhood the terrible duppies of Haiti and Jamaica? Cauls have been powerful preventive magic from pre-history. Cold iron and fairies' knots come, I read, from Cornwall and the fey, strange West Country of England and were old before the Romans arrived. I don't know how those things got transmuted to a small town twenty miles outside Atlanta in the early forties. But I think they were part of that same old, old cloth.

This strange other world our blacks passed to us overlapped the candy-box, *Broadman Hymnal* world of God and Jesus and the Bible so comfortably that children and Negroes could pass from one to another as naturally as between two rooms. To gaunt, gold-toothed Theopal, to huge, magnificent, yellow Mary Elizabeth, to shining-black loving Nellie, and to me, it was entirely possible—though it never happened— to look up from shelling peas on the back porch and see a guppy, or the woman whose head was on fire, or Jesus. Any of the three would have frightened us beyond recall. Theology and the supernatural comforted and terrified child and black equally and alternately, and even if I missed the point of the former back then, I miss the certainty of both now.

It's strange to me that my town didn't have any ghosts: that is, no shades of people who had actually lived, no houses haunted by former tenants. The town, being old and Gaelic in its roots, was ripe for them; the immediate area, being in the path of Sherman's march to the sea, should have had at least one specter, Blue or Gray. One belle in ghostly crinoline, crying around the blackened midnight chimneys for her slain lover and burned world. One haunted, decimated regiment to flash soundlessly over the rattling old wooden bridge that still stands on the road to Jonesboro and Lovejoy Station, where so many Confederates died gallantly and senselessly. And indeed, a little town down the road had an antebellum White Lady, and one to the west had, for some reason, the ghost of a Civil War dentist who was said never to have seen combat duty. But all Fairburn could lay claim to was transparent animals, obscure African elementals, and lights and cold spots.

We had one Thing, though, that was the pride and terror of the entire countryside and had been for many generations: the only manifestation I have ever heard an adult give the time of day to. But a lot of them did, in my childhood, and maybe some still do. It was the Crumpton Booger.

The Crumpton Booger was a thing that had the long, low body of a gigantic dachshund, the legs of a horse, the head of a steer, and the tail of a lion. I think you could interchange the parts however you liked, but those were the only component animals I ever heard mentioned. He had, moreover, red eyes that glowed in the dark and an unearthly scream that, if you heard it, meant an immediate demise in your family. When Hazel MacLaren's father died on the eve of Pearl Harbor, there were people throughout the neighborhood who heard the Crumpton Booger screaming in the night from the roof of the old MacLaren home place. Hazel herself, having been dispatched to a neighbor's house when it appeared her father was dying, saw it, crouched by the chimney against the star-chipped December night, its steer's head thrown back, and heard it scream. She was an immediate celebrity in the third grade.

The Crumpton Booger hung out at a ford in the Chattahoochee River to our west, or else on the piney far shore of Dixie Lake just up the Roosevelt Highway, where we picnicked in the summers. Unlike the Dog, it had no compunctions about getting its feet wet. It was given to chasing people driving the river road in open buggies after sundown, maddening horses and people equally. It could move faster than any horse alive, and more than one good buggy horse was said to have been so fear-crazed after a nocturnal gallop with the Crumpton Booger that he turned bad and had to be shot. My own grandparents have told me about the Crumpton Booger, on nights when we sat around the fire in their parlor and the wood box in the corner turned huge and shadowed with a dancing old darkness.

"I never did pay it no mind," my grandmother would say, searching the embers to see if the verity of the thing lay there, "but my papa always did tell me my uncle Luther—or maybe it was Cousin Boas—was comin' home from courtin' over to Carrollton one night and the thing come up out of the river and got to chasin' him, and caught up to him, and tried to climb right in the buggy with him. He beat it off with the buggy whip."

To have a Crumpton Booger Incident in your own family—that was truly a wonderful thing, and went a long way toward buying a fat, shy, bookish child some glory in a world of sinewy farm kids who could belt a softball a country mile. I told the tale long after I'd lost the baby fat and become a cheerleader and forgotten the Dog. Somehow, the Crumpton Booger was exempt from the banishment of our growing up. He was more a town monument.

Indeed, I trotted him out for author David's inspection that Sunday in the deli after *The Exorcist*. "You people had yourselves a watered-down, regional griffin there, with a banshee thrown in," he said judiciously. "It's really wonderful how pure these old superstitions manage to stay after being handed down through a hundred generations, and crossing oceans. They really don't change, essentially. Old Uncle Luther was probably full of the poteen, but your Crumpton Booger definitely belongs in a collection, something like *The Golden Bough*."

Perhaps he's right. On the other hand, no Minnesota transplant is going to call my great-great-uncle Luther a liar, and he's not going to banish my Crumpton Booger to some anthropologist's desiccated journal, either. Not and get away with it.

"How are the sales on your book going?" I purred creamily. "I was afraid, after those reviews . . ."

Ten Days That Shook
the World

L ast Fourth of July weekend, my husband's four
boys came to visit us. They are now twenty-two,
nineteen, seventeen, and sixteen, tall, straight, sturdy
kids with thick, shining hair and remarkably good
manners compared to the assorted male young who
people my everyday world. To my mind, they are very
beautiful kids, though that appellation would appall
them. They are also frighteningly bright, each in his
own way, and I expect that I'm as besotted with them
as any childless second wife who doesn't see her husband's offspring very often.

They visit about once a year, and it's been fun to
watch them grow into the nice young men they are.
Oh, they've shared a few of their phases with us—the
plaster-cracking drums and rock band bit, from Lee,
the daydreaming oldest. The wily manipulation of his
siblings into furious, red-faced quarrels by Kemble,
the next oldest, who would then sit back with a
detached, seraphic smile on his Botticelli-angel face,

savoring his handiwork. There was a time when we thought Kemble would either be president or a convicted felon by the time he attained his majority. Now, I suppose, it's possible to be both.

Ricky went through a maddening year or so of swinging his arms, cracking his knuckles, shuffling his sneakers, humming tunelessly under his breath, and staying in perfect, perpetual motion. The Rubber Man, we called him. David, the grave, gruff-voiced youngest, displayed a judicial talent for arbitration and peacemaking that was both amusing and touching in one so young. As far as I know, David never had a phase.

But none of the others' phases and quirks ever really bothered me, not even the uncanny ability each still has to eat seven hot dogs at a sitting and go through a dozen family-size Coca-Colas in a day. "Eat, eat," I croon at them whenever they come, turning into the ghastliest Jewish mother imaginable. "You're all skin and bones, eat."

The boys and I have a good working relationship now, having pretty well settled our various roles. When I first met them, they didn't know what to call me. "Mother," of course, wasn't true, and I wasn't quite old enough to have been a natural mother to the oldest two, anyway. "Mrs. Siddons" was patently absurd and stuck in their throats, and they had not been reared to call adults by their first names. They avoided calling me anything when at all possible, and when it was impossible, they addressed me as "Hey," or "mmfff." "Please call me Anne," I pleaded, and finally they were able to do so. We like each other now, and I'm comfortable enough with them to administer an occasional reprimand when their father isn't around.

But it wasn't always so. Their first visit was an ordeal by fire for them and me. We were terrified of each other.

They arrived less than a week after we'd moved into our house, less than a year after we'd been married. Atlanta was in the middle of a long, humid spell of July cloudiness and intermittent afternoon thunderstorms. Doors and drawers were swollen shut, shoes were mildewing in closets, and we hadn't finished unpacking. By hastily assembling an ancient, parent-bequeathed double bed and renting two roll-away cots, we could at least provide the four with beds, but that was about all we had to offer in the way of amenities. The two unused back bedrooms designated for them were cooled by thumping, elderly window units that had two settings—off and high. "They'll never be able to sleep," I fretted. "They'll sleep," said Heyward. "You can't wake Lee and Kem before noon with a jackhammer."

Driving out to meet their plane, I was as dry-mouthed and nervous as if I were on my way to be presented at St. James's. I had made careful plans to become instantly the most perfect proxy mother in Christendom—a combination confidant, culture maven, gourmet chef, and pal. We were going to Read Together and Discuss Our Books afterward. We were going to have inventive little dinners designed to nudge young palates toward New Experiences. Together we would explore the still-unknown woods and creeks behind our house, learning about the birds and small animals there. We would visit the galleries and see the educational films at the library. I rattled all this to Heyward on the way to the airport, finishing up with "There's a wonderful Rauschenberg retrospective at the museum. I think they'll enjoy it."

"I think you're bananas," said Heyward. "You're going to like them, but you're not going to get them within four miles of a museum. For God's sake, relax. They're only kids."

And so they were, when we collected them; kids eight to sixteen, slender children with large, watchful eyes and carefully blank faces and ridiculously small behinds in blue jeans and large feet in Keds. Kids clutching baseball gloves and comic books and one enormous, shining set of drums. Kids like anybody's. To me, they might have just stepped off a space ship from a distant star.

"Welcome to Atlanta," I bleated heartily and falsely. "You're going to love it here."

"Hi. We lived here for seven years. I have to go to the bathroom."

Right away, the gremlins struck. I was taking a week of my vacation to be home with the four, and Heyward had the first four days of their visit free. On the morning of the first day, his office called: Sorry, but there was trouble with a film in L.A. and he'd have to go out and edit. It shouldn't take more than four days. The children and I looked fishily at each other. "If you get any lip from anybody, just whack 'em and put 'em under house arrest," said my husband, dumping clothes into a suitcase. "Jesus, Anne, don't cry. Surely you can manage four *children*."

Surely I could not. The minute he left, the poor kids, smelling raw fear like wild colts, went berserk. And the rains came, and stayed ten days.

I had already learned one thing. My little New Experience dinners for them were going to be New Experience dinners for me. Children live on bland, white, soft things like bread and doughnuts, fried things like potato chips and Fritos, cloyingly sweet things like maple syrup on Twinkies, and do not dig oregano. Moreover, they do not eat the *same* things. Hot dogs for one required ketchup and mayonnaise; for another, A-1 sauce and mild chili; for another, sweet relish and Mister Mustard; and for still another, melted Cheez Whiz. Mushrooms and onions were matter-of-factly picked out of everything and laid ostentatiously on plates. "Yuck, what's that thing?" shrieked one, picking an anchovy off a pizza when I cravenly took them all to lunch the first day. "Got any strawberry Kool-Aid?" said another, foraging in a refrigerator full of fruit juice and milk. One put ginger ale on his Rice Krispies. Silently abandoning Nutrition and praying nobody would get pellagra or scurvy, I sat them down, took grocery orders from everybody, and went off to the supermarket to spend $56.98 on junk.

It was a week spent in the car. In the car in the rain. After the first bored morning scuffle, during which I parroted inanely, "Let's be gentlemen, okay?" I abandoned Discipline along with Nutrition and became a Chauffeur. Mornings we spent at the Lenox Lanes, bowling and playing the pinball machines. I hope never to enter another bowling alley. Afternoons, we went to the movies. In transit, they fought in the back seat and I tried to avoid killing us. After the movies, in the late afternoons while I assembled four sets of whatever carbonated and starch-clotted swill they were dining on, they fought over who was going to watch what on the television set. All except Lee, who dropped out early in the game and took to playing his drums in the back bedroom. I didn't blame him. "We wouldn't fight so much if we had a nice game we could all share," said Kemble helpfully. "Maybe a baseball game or something. I saw a neat one at the Hobby Shop over at Lenox." I went and bought the nice game. They fought over who went first.

By the third afternoon, we had run out of movies I thought it proper for them to see. "John Wayne's on downtown in *The War Wagon*," offered Ricky. "It's just a Western, you know; we're allowed to see Westerns at home." So we plowed downtown in the rain to see *The War Wagon*.

The War Wagon, I discovered after paying ten dollars to get us all in, had more blood and gore than the Somme, and Raquel Welch. Raquel Welch in nothing above the waist. I was quite certain I had violated the What-We're-Allowed-to-See-at-Home code, and equally certain I had done some irreparable Freudian damage to them that would only surface years later. I peered around at four faces, to see if I should drag them out that instant. Lee had gone out for popcorn. Ricky was asleep on my shoulder. Kemble was engaged in trying to pry chewing gum off the back of the seat in front of him. David had to go to the bathroom. So much for blood and bosoms. From then on, we saw every adult Western that hit town.

Things Happen to children with appalling regularity. Kemble developed an inflamed, ingrown toenail and spent a great deal of time soaking it in epsom salts and wondering if he should call home to see what to do. David ran into a guy wire holding up a sapling in the parking lot of the stadium, where we'd gone to see the Braves play, and laid his forehead open. He wondered if he should call home to see what to do. Ricky bumped his head on the bottom of a neighborhood swimming pool and half drowned himself, and wondered if he should call home to see what to do. Lee got a cold. Wondering helplessly what their mother would possibly think of me if this litany of maiming and malaise started pouring in over the wire to Orlando, I suggested that we could probably deal with the carnage ourselves without worrying their mother half to death. "Well, then," said David, admiring his bandaged forehead in the mirror in the dining room, "let's call Dad. *He*'ll know what to do." "I know what to do," I said firmly. "I'm not going to let any of you die."

But once, I thought I was. One afternoon, David came drifting wanly in from the yard, where they'd been halfheartedly tossing around a baseball between thunderstorms. "I don't feel so good," he said. "I feel like I might be getting spinal meningitis." I took his temperature. It was 103 degrees. I ran for the phone and called our doctor.

"I think I have a child here who's getting spinal meningitis," I babbled to the eminently sane, lovely man who is our friend as well as our physician. "Oh?" he said. "What makes you think so?" "He says he is," I wailed witlessly. "And his fever is out of sight." "What is it?" asked Jack reasonably. "One hundred and three degrees," I shouted. "Should I get him down to Piedmont Emergency?"

"Look, Anne, have you got any Scotch?"

"YOU ARE NOT GOING TO TELL ME TO GIVE SCOTCH TO A CHILD WITH SPINAL MENINGITIS," I roared.

"No," said Jack patiently. "I am going to tell you to have a stiff Scotch and water and give the kid two aspirin and put him to bed for a little while. Take his temperature in an hour or two and call me back if it's still up. I don't think it will be." It wasn't.

A restored David was 98.6 in two hours, ate four hot dogs for supper, and participated in the post-dinner fight with glee and gusto.

Wanting terribly to be Loved and Admired, I had applied no discipline to anybody all week. I didn't really know how to scream at kids and was afraid I would find that, when I did, nobody would pay the slightest attention anyway, and the terrible fact that they were In Charge would be out in the open. So the fights escalated all week, with me mewling at intervals, "We just won't be able to go out to Six Flags tomorrow if we're not gentlemen." We weren't gentlemen, and we went to Six Flags. But I was getting haggard and gaunt and noise-shocked, and was beginning to cry a lot. Heyward's four days on the Coast turned to seven, then eight. "Oh, we're all fine," I would bellow into the phone when he called, "everybody's having a wonderful time." Why he bought it I'll never know, since the roars of outrage and blood lust must have carried clearly over the phone to Los Angeles. But he seemed to. "I knew you could handle them," he'd say, and, "Oh, sure, no sweat," I'd lie back.

On the teeming morning of the eighth day, with Heyward due back in the afternoon, a particularly robust fight broke out in the living room. I glanced in and saw one of them swinging a Polynesian war club somebody had given us for a housewarming present in a murderous arc around his head, missing brothers and *bibelots* by inches. Something snapped in my head like a rubber band.

"THE NEXT ROTTEN KID THAT OPENS HIS MOUTH IS GOING TO GET TAKEN APART!" I heard a disembodied fishwife voice screaming very far away.

Instant silence. Utter, complete, blessed, unheard-all-week silence. We stared at each other, frozen in our respective tracks. Well, I've blown this one, I thought drearily. They'll never like me after this.

"Hey," said Kemble. "I've got a dollar saved up from my allowance. If you'll take us to McDonald's, I'll buy you a hamburger."

They were perfect the rest of the week. Angels. They told their father when he came in that evening that they'd never had a better time, and could everybody come back next summer? Heyward beamed around his warm world of clean, happy children and freshly washed-and-dressed wife. "I think you must be a born mother," he said.

A few days later, they called their mother to tell her when their flight was getting in the next day. "Oh, yeah, neat," I heard one of them say. "We got to do a lot of stuff, and saw a naked lady in a movie, and Anne didn't make us eat salads or anything the whole time." I started for the den to cut the treachery short. "Yeah," went on the junior Judas, "and Rick got this little concussion in the swimming pool, and Kem's toe was infected but he didn't get blood poisoning yet, and David cut his head open and got spinal meningitis but he's over it, and . . ."

I stopped in mid-sprint. Heyward was looking at me whitely. "Spinal meningitis?"

"What's a mere trifle like spinal meningitis to a

born mother?" I snapped. "I'm going to have two Scotches and go to bed. You can put out dinner. It's this little thing I whipped up called fried swill. You're going to love it."

Two Weeks in Maine

In August of the year the boys first visited, Heyward took me to Maine for the first time, to decompress and get acquainted with the little summer colony on Penobscot Bay that has been part of his life since he was born. It's an August ritual for us now, maybe the most cherished two weeks of any summer, both slothful retreat and exotic adventure to a Georgia girl whose oceans and seacoasts are tepid, almost tideless water and flat gray sand beaches.

Maine enthralled me totally from the first time I stepped off the Northeast jet from Boston at the quonset hut grandly known as Bangor International Airport. "Please don't judge the rest of Maine by Bangor," said Heyward, as we steered our Hertz rental Plymouth through the scabrous streets of the city. A Victorian city of looming, windowless, red-brick mills and factories that reminds me for some reason of Fall River, Massachusetts (which I've never seen), Bangor isn't a pretty town. But it wasn't like any other place I'd ever seen, either, and the indescribable pine-wine air of Maine had managed to seep inland to Bangor, though smoke and automobile exhausts had diluted it.

"What's the matter with Bangor? I *like* Bangor. Maine is great."

"You like anywhere that isn't home," said Heyward. "Just wait."

So, after a fifty-mile drive through small towns that began to look increasingly like Peyton Place as we neared the coast, we turned left off the pitted black-top at an old white sign that read CENTER HARBOR YACHT CLUB and down a graveled road into Haven Colony. "Oh," I said in pure delight, "it's a hundred years ago."

Haven Colony is almost that old. It was first settled by a group of federal judges from Washington, Heyward's grandfather among them, as a refuge from the Turkish bath that is summertime Washington. Most of the prim, square, gray- or white-shingled cottages went up then, lining a small nest of dirt roads etched through the black evergreens and white birches that slope down to meet the piled boulders of the bay. In those days, people got to Haven via a train to Boston, a steamer to Rockland, and another steamer which wallowed up to the wooden dock at the foot of the bluff and disgorged its passengers before plying off up the coast to Bar Harbor. Some of the more affluent original summer people sent their carriages and drivers and servants ahead and were met at the dock and driven to one rambling two-story cottage or another. Others walked. Then, Haven had stables for summer horses, a central dining hall, and an unpretentious wooden structure on the water named Center

Harbor Yacht Club but called, as it is now, the Club.
The Club is the only one of the original amenities left,
and looks, I'm told, almost exactly as it did in the
1890s.

There's a good clay tennis court now, impeccably
kept up by the summer people and used by the grandchildren and great-grandchildren of the judges. The
superb deepwater harbor beyond the yacht club is
dotted each summer with graceful sailboats bobbing
at anchor, sleek and white and fiberglassed and elab-
orately gadgeted, with one or two elegant old Friend-
ship sloops dreaming magisterially among them.
When they ride idle in the frisking water, sails furled
and slender skeletons of masts white against the
black-green islands, they are incredibly beautiful, and
when they come fleeing home after a regatta, flying
full suits and spinnakers before a freshening salt
wind, you lose your breath.

But it was the old cottages that smote me then,
and still do. They sit center-square on small green
lawns, many girdled with walls of piled gray stones,
and they're shuttered and gabled and chimneyed and
winged and elled, canopied with close-leaning evergreens and mantled with lilac bushes so old they have
become trees. Most are not really large but are
designed to sleep small squadrons of people. One or
two *are* enormous, and even grand, with plush lawns
and rioting rock gardens that bespeak gardeners, and
tall poles from which the Stars and Stripes snap
smartly in the wind off the bay. But most are just
comfortable.

The old house Heyward brought me to, where his
grandparents and parents spent their summers (and
he had, until he went away to the Army Air Corps),

welcomed me as openly as my parents-in-law, who
were smiling from the front door in the chilly blue
dusk. In a flash of déjà-vu, I knew before I entered
that there would be white wicker furniture and birch
logs whispering in a fireplace; a sunporch full of light
and geraniums and old paperbacks; deep-quilted beds
up under the eaves; throw rugs and old pottery. I
knew I would wake on cool, sunny mornings to the
dancing blue stipple of reflected light off the bay on
the ceiling, and grow languid and dreaming and
ignored by time in the crystal air that is unlike any I
have ever smelled.

"I *hope* you like it," said my mother-in-law anx-
iously. "Of course, we're used to it, but it's really
almost primitive. The downstairs bathroom . . ."

But it seemed that my skin already knew the pur-
pling, puckering morning baths in the claw-footed
old bathtub, before the little electric heater revved
up, and my heart and soul had moved in before my
feet got me into the living room.

People don't do much of anything at Haven. Or
rather, they do whatever they wish to do, and that
doesn't seem to include the hectic rituals of oiling,
basking, swimming, tennis, golf, cocktails, dinner,
and so on that flourish in most seaside resorts. Haven
isn't a resort. It's a miniature neighborhood, an old
and mellow one. Most of the people who summer
there are older, and have their own graceful routines
of living. Mornings spent in an unhurried round of
food-gathering, perhaps, down the coast to Dave's
General Store for staples, over to the Vegetable
Lady's or the Egg Lady's; into movie-set little Blue
Hill for library books or a trip to the drugstore.
Lunch on shaded porches. A walk down to the Club,

or a drive into Ellsworth or Bar Harbor, if something as exotic as a new pair of sneakers or a lawn mower part is needed. Naps. Cocktails at neighboring cottages, a stroll home in the rapidly chilling twilight, birch fox fire gleaming eerily in the blackening woods. Supper. A book, or flickering, 1950s TV from Bangor. Early bed.

Visiting young adults play tennis and sail and hike and pick blueberries and antique-prowl, trying to store up enough Maine in their two weeks to get them through their city winters. Or they try to; something in the blue-edged days and the air stuns the most energetic of them into languor after three or four days. It is simply not possible to hurry in Maine. Not to me, anyway. Not now.

My first summer there, however, I whirled at and nipped into everything I could touch in this strange northern summer world. The arm of Penobscot Bay that curls around the colony is called Egemoggin Reach, and I was avid to get down to it, to scramble on its boulders and poke around its seaweed-festooned pebble beach, to swim. Heyward went grumbling with me in the twilight down the steep cliff path behind the cottage to the scrap of boulder-dwarfed beach. Dots of black-pined islands pricked the flat sunset smear of the reach; gulls wheeled and mewled most satisfactorily overhead. A lone sloop was ghosting home out of the fog that was coiling up the reach from the open sea, five miles away. Across the reach, on a distant slick of pink beach, someone was digging clams. A bell buoy sang off around a jog of the reach. "Fog buoy over at Stonington," said my husband. "The fog comes down before you know it. Come on, we'd better get up that path while we can still see. I'm freezing."

I was, too, even in corduroy pants and a heavy sweater. But, "Let me just get my feet wet," I pleaded, and waded into the reach. I was immobilized up to my hips before I even felt the cold. It literally burned, up to my ankles, and I tottered on numbed, clumsy feet up the path to the cottage, hanging on to my husband's hip pocket in the now-descended solid shroud of the fog. When I held my feet up to the fire in the living room, they were a boiled white-red, and I slept that evening in socks. The next morning I saw brown children swimming from the beach and wondered why they were still alive.

On the next afternoon, I encountered for the first time the Down East accent of the true Maine native. I had better luck communicating in Europe. I was taken to be presented to Mrs. Prudence Sylvester, who operates the gas station up the main road into Blue Hill, and I still have no idea whether she welcomed me or maligned me. My treble drawl is nothing against the rock-ribbed, laconic litany of Maine. It took me almost an hour to order rat cheese and grapefruit down at Dave's, and then another of the Summer People, taking pity on me, had to interpret. "Well, they-ah," said Dave, consolingly. "Whey-ah?" I said in unconscious imitation. This is just something Dave says, and requires no reply. "It's a nice morning, Dave," you say, and Dave says, "Well, they-ah."

"What is 'they-ah'?" I asked my father-in-law when I finally reached home with the cheese and grapefruit.

"Oh, Dave," he said. "He means, 'Well, *there.*' You know, like 'There, there now.'"

It's not an accent that can be properly imitated,

though a lot of stand-up comedians seem to try, and my husband will sometimes trot out his version of it at parties, after a couple of drinks. Our friends, never having heard the real thing, usually think it's very clever. The nearest I can come to it is the Hattie Eatus story. This is a treasured old bit of Haven lore and is retold to first-timers with glee. It seems that there was once a cottage down the way with the peculiar name of Hattie Eatus. Most of the cottages once had names; my husband's grandmother, Mother Harriet, named the Siddons cottage "The Milton," but the grandiose appellation died with her and is only a joke now. "Who was Hattie Eatus?" I asked innocently, biting. "Well," said Big Heyward with relish, "the family who lived in the cottage were having a party one weekend, and when the fishman came by, they ordered an unusual lot of fish. He said, 'You folks must be hattie eatus,' and they thought it was so funny they named the cottage Hattie Eatus." I looked blank. "Hearty eaters," said my husband kindly. "Hattie Eatus. See?" I did, finally.

Those first two weeks were idyllic for me; every visit is. Being naturally bone-lazy, I tennis not, nor do I sail. I sit in the ancient wicker chaise on the sun porch, staring at the face of the reach and reading crumbling, yellow Mary Roberts Rinehart novels. I eat prodigiously of clams and lobsters just taken from the bay at Eaton's on Little Deer Isle. I amble the stony, forested paths around the Club and the harbor, revel in the buoy-booming fogs, snooze in front of the birch logs each evening, prowl with Heyward through town after white-steepled little town. I sleep more in two weeks than I do in two months at home, and grow rounder and drowsier each day. The ranks of the summer people have long since welcomed us with cocktails and small dinner parties; I know them now, when I meet them on a morning's foray down to the reach or at Candage's Hardware Store in Blue Hill. Summer Maine is very real to me.

I don't suppose the natives will ever be, though. Civil and accommodating, they nevertheless do not open themselves far to the summer people. Walnut-brown and leathered and taciturn, they seem to me as fixed and silent as their immaculate, stark farms and granite-spined pastures. Maine is a poor state; a bad year for lobsters or potatoes is tangible tragedy. And while Haven is old enough, and its people familiar enough, not to be viewed as a mere source of sustenance, it is that, too, undoubtedly. I don't suppose any people ever really loved their benefactors; I often wondered what those tough, still-faced, dignified people *did* love. Or if they did. I was dangerously close to relegating them to the blithe status of stereotypes.

One evening after dinner, before the fire at a neighboring cottage, someone told me the story of Miss Charity Snow. From time out of mind, Haven had had a post office of its own, a minuscule, one-room white structure with a spotless enameled flagpole and an American flag always square in the bay wind. From time out of mind, Miss Charity Snow had been its postmistress. She was a spare, starched, erect maiden lady, elderly and rooted for generations back in the hard Maine earth. She lived in a tiny white house beside the post office, and her post office was her joy and her life and, even more important, her appointed Work. Miss Charity knew

three generations of summer people and took pride
in never misplacing anyone's mail, be he an original
settler or first-time visitor. Her stamps, waiting to
be sold, were lined in T-square-edged rows and
rolls, and her coin wrappers were dusted every
morning after she'd swept the faultless floor. She
blacked her potbellied stove once a month and
solemnly lowered the flag just at sunset each
evening, consulting her time-and-tide chart to be
sure of the exact moment.

During the Eisenhower administration, the Postal
Department set about consolidating and weeding out
the post offices which were not pulling their weight.
Haven's was one of the nation's smallest, if not *the*
smallest. No one was ever sure. Moreover, it did
appreciable business only in the summer months,
when the summer people were in residence.

Miss Charity Snow got the word on an early
September day. As she had done each evening for
probably fifty of her seventy-odd years, she
realigned her stamps and money orders, swept her
floor, consulted her time-and-tide chart, lowered
her flag, and folded it precisely. The next morning,
an early lobsterman, come to mend his pots, found
Miss Charity Snow's body bobbling gently in the
"flat ca'm" of the dawn reach, half in the water and
half out.

Haven hasn't had a post office since; a fine,
small new one was built in Brooklin, three miles
up the Blue Hill road, and it is a neighborly, effi-
cient place to collect the mail and the out-of-town
newspapers and swap small talk with people from
the colony. I don't like to go there, viewing it
obscurely and romantically as the instrument of

the death of a proud old Down East woman I never even knew.

I still don't know the natives of Maine, and probably never will.

But I know that they love.

The Day the Heat Left Town

Always, when we come home from Maine, the heat surprises me. It has, for two weeks, been totally forgotten in that green-black, cameo-carved world. But it meets you at the airport like a wet dog, and you find you have remembered it viscerally.

I don't think anybody who panted and sweltered through it will soon forget the celebrated heat wave of summer, 1974. It was a heat wave in the classic Georgia tradition, one to recall the shimmery Augusts when we were children and there were not the air-conditioned respites of glacial offices and after-work bars; a heat wave to set our parents and grandparents reminiscing about heat waves past and out of our time. It seemed to me, caught for the first truly hot summer since I left college in unair-conditioned living quarters, a return to a sort of frontier summer that I never knew existed, except atavistically.

What helpless creatures we are, really. Uncomfortable climatic didoes come close to incapacitating us.

After the previous winter, I acknowledged that I was no good in the face of ice. Tornado weather admittedly makes a fool of me. But I had coped with Georgia summers longer than I care to admit. It was just that we hadn't really had one in a long, long time.

When we moved into our house, we bragged a little about the fact that we had no air-conditioning. "We simply don't need it," I was fond of saying, sitting in the dim, cool, tree-shaded living room. We pointed out to whoever would listen the natural superiority of windows open to the fresh, rain-washed air, the sound of twilight bird songs, and the sturdy gurgle of the creek pouring in our windows. "Nature provides all the air-conditioning you need, if you leave the trees standing," I remember intoning pompously to someone on one of our last cool summer nights before we left for Maine.

And some obscure household god who is the natural enemy of domestic pomposity apparently was listening, and put me down in his little black book for a leveling measure of retribution. In August, when the temperature crept stolidly into the low hundreds and dug in for almost a month, our naturally air-conditioned retreat became a blast furnace. The air in our living room promptly became a first-rate sauna bath. Guests, invited for dinner, muttered about erratic babysitters and escaped, still brushing crumbs from their fast-wilting bibs. Plants drooped and died before our eyes. Doors swelled, windows stuck fast, mildew flourished like penicillin. The kitchen became a chamber of horrors. By shutting off every room except our bedroom, with its clangorous window unit, we were able to create one reasonably cool oasis, and we promptly moved into it for the duration.

It was like living for a month in a small Howard Johnson motel room. The television set was ensconced on a leather hassock in the middle of the floor, where it competed with the braying air conditioner for our attention. I crept into the kitchen at intervals and flung together tepid meals of tuna fish salad—or chicken salad, or shrimp salad, or cold soup—and we ate them on trays in the bedroom. The three cats moved in with us, willing to declare a moratorium on their running hostilities until it got cooler. They became languid and fat on tuna fish. Books and newspapers overflowed shelves, tables, bureaus, and dressing tables. We slept a lot, quarreled a little, swatted hot, heavy cats off us, and saw every movie in town.

The greatest weapon a heat wave has going for it is tenacity. There are no distinct days, no orderly progression of time and events. Like severe pain that lasts and lasts, it becomes an entity in itself, a thing that submerges will, personality, ambition, forethought into dumb rote submission. You live in it, like underwater things. Tuesday isn't Tuesday any more. Tuesday is the day it was 101. Wednesday is the day it made 103.

And it is a great leveler. Everybody talks about it, in a listless, mesmeric chant. Watergate, the energy crisis, kidnapings—everything that in a more temperate time would be fodder for brisk conversation—recedes to a point beyond the iridescent bubble of the heat, waiting to be dealt with when things become clear and sharp again, real again.

Downtown is jellied in the heat like consommé. Encapsulated like a marionette theater. Heat swarms in viscous coils from the sidewalk, eddies cobralike in layers at crosswalks, retreats sullenly before futile little gusts from opened doors. People move in the peculiar rigid gait of driven animals, looking neither right nor left nor up—except to confirm the outrage of the heat by the bank thermometer. Dispirited secretaries on their window-shopping rounds give up and *click-clack* back to their offices, depressed and intimidated by the clarion banners of tweeds and tartans in shop windows. The thought of muffling tweed is faintly nauseating. The jaunty bus driver no longer bothers to ask you if it's hot enough for you. The gospel shouter in the downtown park makes no new and joyful noise unto his Lord.

Then one day, when undulating sidewalks and wet, swimming air have always been, will always be; when the salt trickles under your clothes and the thumping air conditioners have so long been parcel and cadence of your existence that silence reverberates, the heat wave totters, snarls, and breaks. This year it came with a rain. Not the brackish, fretful spatter wrung from swollen copper clouds that came every evening during the Heat. A real rain. Clean and forceful, decisive and cold. With thunder immediate and terrible from boiling clouds, and a scourging, avenging wind from some faraway Canadian peak. A wind first to tickle and shiver, then lash and drive the pallid trees, to summon from them the great, shouting chorus they had almost forgotten. An anthem to wetness, coolness, the breaking of the drought, the coming of the fall.

And rain in buckets, sheets, shrouds, waves, the sort that doesn't dawdle but comes swarming down without preface, drenching the matted ghost of grass, the skeletons of shrubs, filling the constricted creek, waking the silent frogs, soaking the restless, sulking cats and sending them bounding and flying home.

It lasted all night. And next morning, there was fall. An edge to things, where none had been for nearly a month. The sun rose low, and there was mist in small hollows, but a white and frosty mist, crystal and definite. When you breathed in, there was a taste and a smell of air and leaves and earth, instead of the metallic wetness of the heat. Sounds reappeared in the new clarity. Doors across the street banged with a definition that brought a senseless and intoxicating joy to ears starved for sharp, clear noises.

It was hot again, of course. Noons burned into still-bare arms, afternoons slept and stirred and slept again. But the Big Heat, the monstrous, torporous animal heat, was gone, and it didn't come back. Mornings were a clear amber brew to send the chipmunks skittering, the birds ruffling and crowing, the cats arching sidewise in tree-scrabbling abandon. The pure, undiluted cobalt that belongs only to autumn stayed in the sky till midmorning. Nights left a frosted sheen on renewed lawns. Wools and tweeds in store windows looked once more like pennons in some tournament meadow at Camelot, gay and valiant and rich.

Caught in the splendid silliness that autumn, more than any other season, works on me, I leaned out my back door and smelled the giddy, head-spinning morning before I left for work. A red leaf, harbinger of the flood that would inundate the lawn in a few weeks, skirled down and was dispatched by the autumn-colored yellow cat, who is fully aware that this coming season is his time of glory.

"I want to go to a football game," I said to my husband.

And that is a sign at our house that the Heat is really and truly gone.

FALL

Fall

∞

"How do you know when fall gets here?" a five-year-old of my acquaintance asked her mother and me on a Sunday afternoon last year. We were sitting on the edge of her parents' pocket-sized swimming pool, dangling our feet in the exhausted September water. The temperature was 92 degrees.

"Fall is when the leaves are red and the air is nippy and you get to wear your new wool clothes," said her mother. "In fact, fall starts officially next week."

The child, taking in the used-green leaves and the heat miasma uncoiling from the patio, clearly regarded this as another piece of adult propaganda and rewarded us with the level stare children reserve for kittenish adult excesses. Wool was a patent insanity in anybody's book, and bright foliage and tart mornings were light-years away from her back yard.

It was most probably a rhetorical question. Children know when autumn comes, almost to the hour. Some small signal forever lost to adults trips the delicate

interior alarm clock that is built into children somewhere behind their ribs. It isn't leaves going bright,
or cool mornings. Those come later. Fall comes when
you stop doing the summer things and start doing the
fall ones.

When I was small, fall came in on roller skates.
Somewhere in the last burning days of August, a
morning came when we met under the oak tree in my
front yard—as we had every morning that summer—
and the skates were there. Jangling in bicycle baskets.
Thumping over skinny shoulders like outsized
epaulettes. Skate keys sprouted amulet-like around
reedy necks, on shoelaces or grimy twine. There had
been no previous agreement to put away the rubber-
tire slingshots and the gut-spilling softballs. The
alarm clock had simply, for each of us, gone off
sometime in the dreamless night.

For the rest of fall, up until the lowering winter
met us on the way home from school and robbed us
of the light, skating was the autumn thing that we
did. We went in swooping flights down sidewalks
and streets, always with our parents' "Be *care*ful!"
thrumming in our ears, drunk on our own momen-
tum, giddy on wind and wheels. The very small ones
of us, restricted to front walks, windmilled on treacherous feet and looked with awe and hate at the flying
phalanxes of big kids streaming by, trailing immortality like a bright comet's tail. The more accomplished
of us were allowed to skate as far as the shuffleboard
court on the high school playground—smooth, seam-
less, utopian skating.

We came to know every street, every sidewalk, by
the burring skirr our skates made on them; they
spoke to us in a hundred voices, through the soles of

our feet. Each of us, every fall, ruined a pair of shoes with too-tight skate clamps. Knees were scabbed until Christmas.

School started somewhere in the yellowing days, and we went back to the rows of scarred desks that left forearms perpetually bruised with the ghosts of last year's ink. We were strange to each other for a little while in those first days, even though we'd been together like litters of kittens for a whole summer. Reluctant to be laid by, the jealous summer still tugged at our hair and tickled behind closed eyelids.

But soon we were the spawn of chalk and cloakrooms again, creatures of a thousand rituals, and the wild summer children were gone. Tans went mustardy and flaked under an onslaught of starch. Big colt's feet, bare and winged like Hermes' all summer, were earthbound as Clydesdales' in clunking new saddle oxfords. Rasping new sweaters began to feel good in the mornings as we jostled and quarreled to school, flanked by an honor guard of trotting dogs. But the sweaters were shed in the still-hot noons and left to grieve in balls, stuffed into our desks. By the time the real cold set in, and the hated coats and leggings were brought out of cedar chests, the sweaters were frail and used, forgotten until spring behind Blue Horse notebooks.

Summer was a time of good things to eat, of course, but it is the taste of autumn that I remember. Wild, smoky, bittersweet things ripened in the bronze afternoons, and the glazed mornings bit them to exotic sharpness. Preposterous yellow persimmons grew on a tree in the schoolyard, and if you got a good one, the taste was incredible, wonderful, like a topaz melting on your tongue. Too-ripe ones were truly dreadful, tasting just like their overripe peers which had burst and gone to yellow slime on the ground looked, sly and sickened. Too-green ones would pucker your mouth to acid flannel for the rest of the day.

Scuppernongs hung on an old broken arbor on my grandfather's farm: huge, green, gold-dusted things that were surely the sweetest fruits autumn ever gave a greedy child. Flinty little Yates apples lay on the ground under the old trees in the ruined orchard, each one worth one bite of pure, winy nectar before you noticed half a worm. Sweet potatoes, newly dug from their sand hills and roasted in my grandmother's black coal stove, were honey and smoke, too rich to finish.

But pomegranates were the Grail.

It seems that pomegranates always hung over my childhood autumns. And they were always forbidden fruit. Just as Persephone was imprisoned six months in the underworld for eating pomegranates, so I was regularly placed under house arrest for stealing Mrs. Word's pomegranates next door. On the outside, Mrs. Word's pomegranates were tough and leathery and rosy and enormous. On the inside, when you broke them open, the rows of rose-quartz crystals were Kubla Khan's toys. I don't think I ever really liked the strange Persian taste of them, but I stole enough of them to keep a Bronx fruit stand in business. Like Everest, they were there. One of the worst moments in my life to this day was the time my mother apprehended me at my black business and marched me, mewling like a cornered kitten, into Mrs. Word's impeccable parlor to confess and seek forgiveness. It was, of course, granted.

As the fall wore on, mornings were born silver, and bleeding sunsets came earlier, and rumbling furnaces came alive in basements. We melted, with a winter-long stench, the soles of our saddle oxfords, standing over hot-air registers. The Southeastern Fair wheeled by in a technicolor blur of sawdust and cotton candy and forbidden midway shows where, the big kids said, ladies took their clothes off. Halloween smelled of the wet, burnt insides of pumpkins and was terrible with an atavistic terror in front of the fire in our living room, where my father read me the witches' speech from *Macbeth*. I remember one magic night in October when I was plucked up out of sleep, wrapped in a quilt, and taken outside in our back yard to watch a meteor shower. Warm on my father's shoulder, but with everything strange and too big and not like our back yard at all, I watched as the very sky above me wheeled and arced and bloomed. It was, I thought, something God arranged for me because He knew my father.

Soon ice crystals bristled in red clay, waiting to be scrunched under the loathsome galoshes. Saturdays and Sundays, which had been vast blue bowls to whoop and tumble in, so full of joy that little gold specks pinwheeled behind your eyelids when you closed them, turned gray and howled. We did smeary things with stubbly, useless scissors and paste—does anyone remember the forbidden peppermint taste of library paste?—and drove our parents wild, whining plaintively about the eternities of our heavy days.

We listened, with much the same look as my young friend beside the swimming pool, to their patient recounting of the fun we'd have next spring, when we could go outside again. But that was next year, a different digit on a new calendar. And between us and spring, as the fall came down like a black window shade, was a long, whirling winter place where anything could happen.

Even Christmas. But that's another story.

The Bad Time

∞

One grape-flushed October evening last year, I got home from work a little later than usual, absently poked the ankle-circling cats with the toe of my shoe, and put my key into the back-door lock. The kitchen was dark, and there was nothing more troublesome on my mind than what to do with the Greenland turbot fillets thawing flaccidly on the drainboard. I do not like fish, but I feel honor-bound to buy it in the interest of economy, and am sorely taxed each time I serve it to devise a sauce that will disguise its origins.

When I flicked on the kitchen light, there was an enormous, radiant bouquet of asters spilling rowdily out of a saucepan, a fifth of Taittinger sweating in an ice bucket, a miniature robin's-egg-blue Tiffany shopping bag sitting in a clutter of mail, and my husband rummaging in the Thing Drawer for a corkscrew.

"We finally got our tax return!"

"No. It's the fourth anniversary of the end of the Bad Time. Don't tell me you'd forgotten."

I hadn't. But I'd buried it so effectively that the mere mention of it made me as sick as if I'd been hit in the stomach with a line drive. I am not gallant and gay and go-to-hell, much as I'd like to be, and remembered travail acquires no gilt edges in my mind. I am a natural-born flincher, and I flinched that evening.

"Oh, God, Heyward, it's bad luck to celebrate bad luck. It's like daring it to come back again."

"You have an interesting mind," said my husband, thunking the cork out of the champagne. "Half Southern Methodist and half Druid. Have some champagne and count your blessings."

So we drank up the champagne that evening, and I arranged my asters and admired my present, and we never ate the turbot. I fed it to the cats. We counted our blessings, and by the time the Taittinger was gone and the litany of present good fortune had reassured and emboldened us, we were able to talk about that seven-month bog of time that started a handful of Februaries ago, which we have come to call the Bad Time.

In early 1970, the economy was struggling in a terrible underwater thing euphemistically called a recession, and things in Atlanta weren't good. Except for Lockheed-Georgia, we suffered no mega-bloodlettings in any particular industry; Atlanta is a branch-office town, not a one-industry town. But our support industries, as the leaf-dry socioeconomists fattening on university grants call them, bled badly. And none so immediately and sanguinely, perhaps, as advertising and its related fields. Advertising is largely a luxuriously parasitical business; when its hosts thrive, it is as fat and shiny as a tick. When its hosts sicken, it does, too. It often dies while its hosts survive. In hard times, only taproots will give sustenance. Advertising lives on the taproots of others.

So, in Atlanta, jobs in advertising were among the first to go. My husband worked for a television production studio that made commercials for advertising agencies throughout the Southeast. I had left my own job as a copywriter in an advertising agency some months earlier, to stay home and do free-lance writing. At that time, the disease that was creeping out of the East and California hadn't reached Atlanta yet. Witlessly watching Heyward's studio thrive in the last feverish flush of ersatz health, watching the bonus checks roll in, I had decided we no longer needed my full-time income. I wanted to stay home for the first time in my adult life and play with my house.

So I was home fiddling ineptly with an old oak chest and an antiquing kit on the Friday afternoon that he came home at three o'clock, still-faced and strange and walking a little stiffly, and told me the studio had folded. He and twenty-odd other people were out of a job.

We should have seen it coming. Perhaps we did. We are alike in that both of us are great not-noticers of omens and storm clouds. Or were then. None of the agencies in town had cut back yet, but the business that served them—the television and recording studios, the talent and model agencies, the typography houses—were quietly letting people go one at a time. These businesses pay their own suppliers out-of-pocket and are then reimbursed by the agencies who hire them. If agency payments are late, the cash flow dries to a trickle. If agency payments stop, the cash flow in these businesses dies. Agencies, caught in their own cash flow crunch from their clients, were beginning to stop paying. And so studios and such were cutting personnel. And then more personnel. And then closing.

Not long after, the great mass cutbacks at the advertising agencies began, and you would hear that so-and-so let nine people go yesterday. They fired fourteen over at such-and-such last Friday. Twenty-two got it at another agency. Some of the smaller ones closed and never reopened. But all that was to come later, and we didn't know about it that February Friday. Oddly, I think it would have helped if we had.

There seem to be several quite distinct stages you go through in an unemployment crisis. The first is exuberance. An idiotic, totally irrelevant gaiety, a near-relief rather like that of hearing that the tests came back positive. "Well, I'm delighted," I said. "I hated that tacky place anyway. They ran it like an operetta. You always were better than they deserved. I'm going to call up some people and ask them for drinks."

All that evening, we were flushed, fevered, hectic, silly. I careened around being the Sweetheart of the Squadron. Heyward was gallant and droll. Our friends were extravagantly supportive. We laughed, danced, drank martinis, ate Chinese take-out food. None of us was ever quite so witty, so gay, so animated. It was very cold at the core of the night.

We made jokes and plans that spiraled upward from mordancy to lunacy. Heyward would go to law school and become a lawyer; he'd always wanted to. Heyward and I would open our own advertising agency; with our combined experience, we would be an instant success. Heyward and I would sell our house and go live off the good earth in the cottage in Maine, a life of quiet contemplation and exquisite small pleasures. We would farm a little, and I would write sensitive, reflective novels, and he would paint. Maybe we'd buy a small weekly newspaper. We would have friends up in the summers and read and listen to Beethoven in front of great roaring birch-log fires in the snow-felted winters.

I think it was this last fantasy that broke the iridescent bubble of shock and let the first of the fear in to stab us. The cottage in Maine is not winterized; we would have frozen to death by mid-November. The soil is three inches deep over solid granite halfway to China. Neither of us can make a terrarium grow. Nobody was buying houses in an economy fluttering wounded toward the earth, and we did not have enough money to buy a small weekly newspaper. We had about enough money to last for two months.

When the last of our friends left, we looked at each other and we went to bed and we held each other and I cried. I was scared to death, frightened with a bone-deep, void-black fear that I had never felt before, a terror that I knew instinctively was not going to go away for a long time, a simple animal terror that could only be expressed as "I do not know what is going to happen to us. I do not have any rules for this."

Stage two consists of making rules. Bones to hang this new entity on. Busy, brisk, no-nonsense plans, a Game Plan. The rules we made were, many of them, as inappropriate and ill-suited to the crisis as that first night of glittering lunacy. But then, nobody knows how to go about being unemployed. Feeling brave and fearless, a Spartan woman, I asked for— and got—a job as a writer-reporter on the city magazine I'd left in the mid-sixties. It paid about half what my carelessly abandoned copywriting job paid, but it was well funded by the Chamber of Commerce and in no danger of folding. It shames me now to admit that I felt strong and free and almost immortal, leaving in the dark mornings, chin lifted to the gales of adversity, to Work and See Us Through, but I did. At first. It wasn't until later that I noticed what was happening to my husband when I brought my paychecks home.

Heyward, left alone in a weekday house where he'd never been unless he was ill, began knitting his own web of days. He called the bank that holds our auto loan, the savings and loan institution that holds our mortgage, the department stores where we have accounts, and told them we would try but there might be a few missed payments. He called the court that administers his child support payments and told them the same thing. All were compassionate. Just keep in touch, they said. He would, he said. But it would probably only be a month or two. There were some excellent prospects.

And there were. The big artery in advertising hadn't been cut yet. Someone would call and say, "I hear they need a broadcast director over at X." "They're looking for an account man at Y." "Z needs a production manager." Heyward called them all. It is not easy to say you are looking for a job because you are out of work in our business. The best jobs go to the ones who are employed and looking for something better.

"We'll let you know," said X, Y, and Z. "Things are tight right now, you know." Most of them never called back. Things were tight.

The days you didn't expect many of wear on, and soon you have a month of them, strung like beads of bright pain. The best leads—the word-of-mouth leads—dwindled and the rounds of employment agencies began. The Big Guns. The management placement services, Select-an-Exec. The ones who convince you that an exquisitely wrought résumé is your key to the kingdom and charge you blind for three sheets of cryptic runes. Let Us Create the Written You. "You should consider another field, Mr. Siddons, with things in advertising a bit iffy right now. With your skills and experience, and our training courses . . ." God, I hated them then for what they were doing to the gentle, talented, productive man who is my husband. I hate them just as much now.

We were still in the hopeful, it's-just-a-matter-of-another-week-or-two phase, and we had odd spells of giddy laughter, great closeness, wild exhilaration, unexplained euphoria. Heyward would pick me up after work and we would drive home together in the pale, beginning-to-be-spring green evenings. We'd have tuna fish casseroles and wine—we refused to let *all* the ceremonies go—and we'd lie jumbled together on the couch watching television, happy and content. Through the whole siege, except for a few murderous explosions, we never lost that skin-to-skin closeness. I don't know why. In the spate of articles that came out during the recession dealing with the human impact of unemployment, I read over and over that it could be one of the most cruelly divisive experiences a marriage can undergo. But we seemed almost totally happy on those evenings. Indeed, sometimes I think wistfully of the simple sharing of the Bad Time. I believe it was because we were down to basics—us—and finding that the basics would hold up.

The days were bad, though, as the string of beads lengthened. They were times of heart-skittering anxiety for me at work—"Did he see the guy at Consolidated? I wonder if the thing with the suburban newspapers came through. Did the man from the TV station call back?"—but I was distracted by my own interviews and deadlines. The days were unmerciful to him.

There are just so many people you can see. So many phone calls you can make. So many contacts. When they're all made, what then?

You wait. He did. Calls came, or didn't come. "We haven't decided." "We *have* decided—we just can't fill that position at the present." "We'll let you know for sure in another week." "Can you call us on Monday?"

We began to treasure the calls that were to come two or three days later, or in a week. They meant that we wouldn't have to worry about the outcome until then. A silent phone was okay; they said they wouldn't call until next week. You could look forward to not looking forward to them.

As the prospects in Heyward's field dwindled, the meanest small jobs began to look feasible. "It would tide us over until I found something I really liked, till the crunch eases up." Then promising. Then precious. Things to be prayed over in eye-squinting agony under the shower. A mean-spirited lout of a prospective employer could become, for a while, the pivot jewel of your future. "Oh, God," I would gargle while scrubbing my back, "please, please let him hear from the man at the discount house advertising department. Today. Not for me, for him. He's tried so hard, and he's so good, and he's so brave, but I know this is killing him. . . ."

But it was me it was killing, not my husband, who is made of rock and knows his own worth. When he worried, it was for me. Superstitious, small-spirited, vain, hand-wringing me. I cringe now, thinking of those mewling prayers.

During the middle of the Bad Time, we hit a sort of stasis. Heyward would make his calls and go to his interviews, but the silent daytime house was beating him into something shyer, smaller, more tentative. "I hate to answer the door when those women come around collecting for things. It ought to be you." He would grin, but it was a rictus of hurt. I began to fathom then what a terrible idiot world it is that denies a man his own house during weekdays from nine to five.

He painted the entire house, inside and out. He fixed gutters, the roof, the wiring in the basement. We both began to parcel out time, to give ourselves small gifts to look forward to, to bisect weeks. A roast for day after tomorrow. A party invitation next weekend. Let's have the Pattersons over, and I'll make chili. But there were more and more times that he didn't want to see his friends who were still employed. I didn't blame him. He had smiled confidently through too many lunches; he had talked matter-of-factly about the prospect he'd be hearing from next Monday at too many parties. One afternoon, I called him from work; he wasn't in. "Where were you?" I asked when he picked me up at work. "I went to a movie," he said. Nothing during the entire Bad Time tore at me any worse, but I still don't know why.

Some of the worst times had wildly funny overtones. My husband in his Brooks jacket and his Princeton tie, standing in an unemployment line. My own hysterics at being told by a neighbor that an orange car had pulled into the driveway one day while we'd both been out, had parked there for a while, and then left. I cried for an hour, sure it was someone come to foreclose on the house. (It was an old friend passing through town, I learned later. "Orange Car" has since become a code word that means "Cool it and quit worrying.")

Some of the worst times were of my own making. Calm, reasonable, supportive, understanding for weeks on end, I would come home and hear my own brittle voice neighing casually, "Did what's-his-name call?"

"No."

"Oh, my God, can't you call *him*? Can't you do *anything* but paint this goddamn house? I can't *stand* this any longer!"

Oh, the little murders. The tiny, erosive outrages of trust and commitment. Slowly sagging under an imbecilic system that insists that what a man works at is his measure, he couldn't even reply.

And some of the worst times had in them such cores of kindness and decency and human magnificence that they shine still for us, and always will. Along toward the end of the Bad Time, our lives had taken on a sort of Pinteresque quality, a Jobian cast. My grandmother died. An elegant, funny Siamese we were keeping for friends was hit by a car. We came home one evening to find we'd had a burglary. God, how we pitied us. But we were laughing by then. There was no valor in the laughter. It was simply visceral reflex.

Then the Major, my stately, green-eyed puff of gray Persian, got very ill, and we took him to the vet. It was feline pneumonitis, a very bad thing and one that cats rarely get over. When they do, it's after a long, long hospitalization. The Major is tough, he was hanging in there, but as two weeks ran into three, and then four, he was over the two-hundred-dollar mark and still racking up the charges. And the vet simply couldn't say when he would be ready to come home. Or if.

There came a Saturday morning when we knew we couldn't pay for him any longer. Heyward hugged me for a long time, and we both cried, and then he called the vet and asked that he put the Major to sleep. "We honestly can't pay you any longer," Heyward said. "I'm not even sure we can pay you what we owe you now."

"This is a neat guy, this old gray tom," said the vet. "He's a fighter. I'm not going to lose this old fellow. There's no charge from here on out."

In some near-mystic way, the vet broke the Bad Time for us. The same tough, cocky, untutored hope we'd had in the first weeks came flooding back. The heat lifted and fall came sharpening into town. Two people called Heyward with job offers: not so hot, but firm. While he was mulling them over, an old friend, a sweet, canny man whose to-the-pointness is legendary, called me at the office. "We're starting a subsidiary advertising agency here at the plant. I'd like Heyward to manage it. Where is he?"

It's where he has been since, and he is most uncommonly good at it, and it is unfolding like a telescope under his guidance, and it is hard for me not to keep thanking John. When I did, the first time, he gave me a mackerel stare and said, "I've never done you any favors. That was business."

Well, and so the Bad Time ended. In retrospect, it wasn't, of course, not really. Compared to some people's Bad Times, it was a stroll through an English garden. We still know nothing of the sort of grinding anguish one does not get over. We have lost no child, had no crippling illnesses, we have not either one lost the other of us. Which is not to say we won't and being, as Heyward says, half Southern Methodist and half Druid, I am so superstitious that I do not even like to write those words.

But on a scale of ten, I'd give our Bad Time a four, and contrary to popular myth, I am sure it did not toughen me, teach me, gentle me, smarten me. I am still mortally afraid of lost jobs and do not wish to weather another. I can find no residual wisdom from that one to carry with me into another. I think that the uses of adversity stink.

I learned a little more about my own private haunts, though. I learned that what I am most afraid of is not what will ultimately happen, but of having to endure the fear. I am afraid of having to be afraid for a long time. I want my fright to be over in the morning. "Okay, God," I bargain smally, "I'll agree to being scared witless, but how about letting it be okay by—say—next Thursday, huh? I'm not good for the long haul."

The man I live with, the one whose shoulders bore it all, did gain from it. "We will make it, Anne," he says, "no matter what happens, unless we screw it up ourselves. I know that that is true."

Me, I need talismans. Wood to knock. New moons to wish on. Cracks not to step on.

And him.

Reflections on Advertising

Every year in mid-fall, the Atlanta advertising community, as it is wont to call itself, meets in a downtown motel ballroom for cocktails, a banquet, and the doling out of awards that it has bestowed on its members during the year past. It is a funny, nepotistic, Flash Gordon sort of affair, and every year I go, along with my peers who write copy or design advertisements, to see if someone has given me a present for being a clever writer. We all purport to scorn this annual mass onanism, but we all go. Public praise is as sweet as Christmas morning to advertising people, me included.

This year's fete was much like every year's. The younger writers and art directors, in dress-up Levi's and a lot of skin and knobby spines, clustering around the bar and wreathed in clouds of "straight" smoke, muttering about the irrelevancy of out-of-town judges. Schools of Braggi-scented account people circling and nibbling like sharks in John Wayne suits. Agency heads nursing drinks and smiling benevolently at Their People at Play, secure and popelike in the knowledge that, for them, the agonies and ecstasies of public competition are past. If their agency doesn't pull in its share of gold medals, it is going to be the creative director and his sullen staff who catch hell at the next agency meeting.

Off in a corner, the Out-of-Town Personage, imported to judge the competition, smiles Buddha-like in a knot of admirers. Usually, he is what advertising people call a "hot creative type" from a fast-blooming New York agency known for its "heavy, gutsy campaigns," whose ads for booze and anti-booze remedies and sometimes even entire countries flower in national magazines and network prime time. He is certain to be outspoken, amusing, arrogant, Italian, and very, very good at his business. He is also short. I have never met a tall Out-of-Town Personage. Before the awards are passed out, he will show slides of his work, and comment on them, and share with the assemblage his rationale for putting them together. He will tell a number of funny client stories—or, rather, tales of how he and his staff managed to create such pearls in the face of incredible imbecility on the part of his Philistine clients—and cadet writers and artists will take notes, and everybody will laugh and applaud.

During his talk, and during the melting-sherbet-and-coffee stage, those of us who haven't snuck out to the bar are rehearsing wry, funny, humble little speeches of acceptance for the upcoming awards, designed to make us shine in the eyes of our peers and to impress the Personage with our spontaneous wit. Perhaps he will call us up next Monday from

New York and offer us a job. More creativity is expended during the pre-award period of an advertising banquet than in maybe six months of typewriter and drawing-board time.

The awards themselves are almost irrelevant. They are endless, and given for such things as "best two-thirds page black-and-white newspaper track ad for package goods" and "best local television campaign consisting of three or more thirty-second spots for financial institutions to run in non-prime time." One by one, the humble creator of each winning entry rises, trots up to the podium, ducks his head, mumbles his shy, creative acceptance speech, is applauded, and returns to his seat, casually placing his gold whatever in the center of the table. The person who has the most gold whatevers clustered around his plate at the end of the evening Wins. Or, rather, his agency does. After the affair is over, the winning agency repairs to the motel bar and is in residence at a large corner table, where losing teams file by to pay homage. Everybody is usually very drunk before the evening is over.

What has always surprised me most about these things is the press coverage they get. There is always at least one camera crew from a local station, and the flash bulbs go off like a little war all evening. Next morning's papers will carry a full account of Who Won, and there will be pictures of humbly grinning awardees and smiling agency heads and the eager-to-be-gone Personage, his drawing arm draped around the prettiest receptionist in the room. It is a combination of the Academy Awards, the Miss America pageant, and a Dale Carnegie graduation. The most eminent surgeons in America, gathering in Atlanta,

don't get this sort of press. Most national political figures don't. When the Organization of American
States met in Atlanta recently, they made page two,
section B. When the ad types gathered this year, page
three, section I, had a headline reading AD COMMUNITY
FETED. Like pandas and lost cats who walk three
thousand miles back to their old homes, I think we
must be natural curiosities.

I don't know of another business (I balk at "pro-
fession," though a lot of us call it that) that is so highly visible. "I'm in advertising," you say to somebody
at a party who has asked you what you do, and you
get one of three basic responses. "You people are
manipulating the consumer. How can you live with
yourselves?" Or, "How interesting. All that money
for thinking up captions for pictures. I've always
thought I'd have made a pretty fair advertising man.
Let me tell you the line I thought up for my brother-
in-law's roller bearing business." Or, "Are all those
stories about what goes on in advertising agencies
true?" (This last with a smoky, half-lidded, sidewise
look.)

There aren't any acceptable rejoinders to the first
two. Advertising people don't think any more about
manipulating consumers than muffler installers think
about manipulating automobile owners, and if they
can't live with themselves, it's usually because they
have said something stupid and mean to their husbands or wives, or didn't tell the lady in the checkout
line she gave them back a ten instead of the one they
had coming. Just like anybody else. To the guy who
has thought up a funny line for roller bearings, you
would like to say, "I don't want to hear it," but you
usually listen politely and smile. Just like anybody else.

But to the last, the answer is an unequivocal "yes." It's true that wild things go on in advertising agencies. Only what goes on is seldom what people think.

Unless you have been in it for forty years or haven't had a vacation in a very long time, advertising has got to seem a funny business. It can also be deadly serious and highly professional, like any other business, and can be as heartbreaking and precarious as any. In the bad money crunch of '69–'70, there were thousands of advertising people out of work, and their families suffered and worried just as much as the families of the men on the GM and Ford assembly lines who were laid off. But advertising has a built-in ludicrous factor going for it, and the best ad people I've ever known are the first to recognize and savor it.

It has, for instance, a language all its own, and it's a very funny language. Some are serious working terms of the trade: "Kill," "bleed," "shoot," "widow," "laid," "strip," "gang," "cut." They all mean something specific that you do to an advertisement in its various stages of production, but to the uninitiated ear, advertising must sound a grim and dangerous business indeed. I know this to be true because of the poor shrink who works down the hall from our office. An art director and I made of him a shattered man in one short elevator ride one fine afternoon.

The shrink is really a family counselor, and he hung out his shiny new shingle about a year ago in the empty offices across the hall from my agency's reception area. He was then a friendly, open-faced man who nodded and smiled when he met one of us in the elevator or on the way to the restrooms. I'm not sure he knew, for a while, what our office did, since the tasteful pewter sign outside our door could as easily designate a law firm or a brokerage house. My art director friend and I came grumbling out of the office, discussing an advertisement we had done for an elegant ocean resort on the Carolina coast, which the client had rejected. The reason for the rejection was that I had caroled lyrically in the copy about riding a horse on the unspoiled, wind-swept beach, and the art director had included a picture of a beach rider on horseback in the ad. The client had pointed out, logically enough, that horses weren't allowed on the beach, as they had a lamentable tendency to crap on it, and then somebody had to go out and rake it up, and if we put it in the ad, some literal-minded guest was going to wave the ad in an executive face and demand to ride a horse on the beach, and the management would have no recourse but to let him.

We boarded the elevator sullenly, deep in rumblings about three weeks' work down the drain, hardly noticing the affable shrink, who got on with us. "Well," said the art director, "I guess you heard that the client killed the horse."

"Oh, damn," I rejoined. "What are you going to do?"

"Well, you're going to have to cut it, of course," he said. "And I'm going to have to go down there next week and shoot another one. It's a goddamn bore."

The elevator lurched to a stop on three, and looking up from our sour musings, we got just a glimpse of white-ringed eyes and shock-slackened mouth as the poor shrink dodged off the elevator and out of the company of the two sociopaths he had thought were such nice, wholesome people. Now he keeps his door closed and carefully pursues the pattern in the hall carpet when we cross paths, restroom-bound. I haven't noticed him working late alone in his office since. He probably prays every night that none of us becomes suddenly violent or certifiable during office hours, so he won't be sent for.

Words are a large part of an advertising agency's stock in trade, and when they are well used, the client's product or service makes money and the client is happy and renews the contract and often ups the ante, which makes the agency happy and is what the business is all about. By and large, the selection and application of proper words is a serious and diffi-cult business and is rarely as fey and "fun" a process as Hollywood, some novelists, and people who want to break into the business seem to think it is. It is fun, but the fun comes, for most of us, after the thing is written and you know you have done a good job on it. Spending three weeks to produce a sixty-page booklet and then having to rewrite it two more times before you've gotten it the way you—or the client— wants it is not only hard work, it's crazy-making. This sort of prolonged siege of concentration on something as nebulous as the inside of your own head is also a fertile breeding ground for errors, which can be harmless or lethal, depending on their context and whether or not somebody notices them before the final product is in print or on the air. Happily, most of them *are* caught and rectified in time, but when they're not, they are worse than relatives who come for a week and stay two years. I am still writing let-ters of apology to people who write to an eminently good-natured and long-suffering client of my agency's in Virginia, pointing out that it was James I who was king of England in 1607, *not* James II. Rarely does a copywriter change the entire course of history.

Errors can be the result of fatigue, sloppiness, boredom, or just the law of averages. One poor copywriter of my acquaintance, trying for the fifth straight day to find a way to say that, at a certain resort, you had your choice of having fun with a lot of people or getting away by yourself—and having space for exactly nine words—triumphantly wrote, "Enjoy other people, or better still, play with yourself." That one got through seven people at her agency and five clients before somebody noticed it, just in time to call the magazine in New York and shout, "Hold it!" Another error that almost streaked meteorlike across the financial pages of both Atlanta's metropolitan dailies was a salute to a group called the Intercontinental Bankers. Only it read, in twenty-four-point type (that's pretty large type), "We salute the incontinent bankers." That, too, was prevented by an eleventh-hour call to the newspaper by our harassed production manager, who was so convulsed with hysterical laughter that he couldn't speak for five minutes. I doubt if the good bankers would have found it amusing.

Sometimes errors are deliberate, the products of late-hour silliness and unfettered, irreverent, creativity rebelling against the strictures of budget, time, and sober purpose. Creative people are funny people, or they wouldn't be doing what they do. And they make superb audiences for each other. So errors of this kind flourish in recording studios and on television locations and sets, where you invariably have, in addition to the people who wrote and art-directed the commercial being produced, the inventive and

talented people who act in them or read them. This
volatile combination is an accident waiting to happen, and coupled with the fact that a great deal of
shooting and recording is done after hours, when
everybody is getting tired and the booze has been
broken out, you get some sublime insanity. You can
also get into deep and abiding trouble.

When I first went to work for my agency, we were
recording a series of seven or eight radio spots for a
client who sold coffee and tea. I was there in the
recording studio because I had written the spots. The
creative director was there because that's what he
does. The two people who were reading my spots
were friends of his, two enormously funny, professional, and talented guys whose readings are impeccable and whose ad libs are genius. Indeed, they're
now head writers for one of the funniest and longest-
running situation comedy series in television, and
have been on the Johnny Carson show and God
knows what else. Funny guys. In those days, however, they hadn't yet been discovered, and because
they needed the money, they would fly into Atlanta
and we would work straight through the day into the
night to wrap up whatever it was we had for them to
record, so they could fly back home.

When you make a mistake on tape, it is called an
outtake. It simply means somebody flubbed the spot,
and the editor will eventually toss it out and not use
it. This day, we had gotten through seven spots and
were slogging into number eight. It was nine in the
evening. We were up to take ninety-seven, and down
near the bottom of a fifth of Cutty Sark. The spot we
were working on involved a precocious child genius
who was being interviewed by a smarmy moderator.

The moderator was supposed to say something like, "Our next guest is little Johnny Smart. Well, little Johnny, and is it true you're only eight years old?" To which little Johnny was to reply, "Yes. You wanna count my teeth?" or some such idiocy.

Wearily, the guy who was playing the moderator said for the seventeenth time, "Our next guest is little Johnny Smart. Well, little Johnny, is it true you're only eight years old?"

"Yes," said the ersatz little Johnny. "Wanna see my dick?"

After we had howled, wept, roared, rolled around on the floor, and played the spot back several times, we got a perfect spot on the ninety-eighth take and wrapped up the session. But everybody agreed that the outtake was too funny to destroy, and that we would have the sound engineer make a dub of it and send it over to the agency the next day, so we could play it for everybody.

It is a grave error not to destroy outtakes, no matter what gems they are. Since the outtake is put into a neat little square white tape box just like the "keeps," it will invariably get played somewhere it shouldn't be heard, simply because somebody is in a hurry and doesn't read the word "outtake" on the label.

Shortly after the Little Johnny incident, a couple of people were putting together a sample reel of radio tapes, which means they splice together the best radio spots the agency has done for the past year or so to play for new-business prospects. This shows businesses who are trying to decide on a new advertising agency the sort of work we do. Approximately four minutes before a particularly toothsome new prospect was due to appear in the conference room,

somebody decided they'd better run the tape, just to
double-check things. Simultaneously with the sound
of our elevator doors rumbling open to spill out the
Prospects came the falsetto voice of little Johnny
Smart braying, "Wanna see my dick?" Mercifully
diverted by our pretty and resourceful receptionist,
they didn't hear the outtake, and the sweating creative director had time to cut it off the master. There
are more of these cliff-hangers in advertising than is
comfortable for any of us, but to most of us they are
very necessary condiments.

The people who work in advertising agencies are
probably not precisely like anybody else, but it's not
always because they are genuine eccentrics. Some of
them are, and I've never decided if the business
attracts eccentrics or creates them. But the noneccen-
tric ones often appear that way because they must
deal seriously every day with essential absurdities.
One of my agency's principals is the sanest, gentlest,
most charming man I shall ever meet, a warm, liter-
ate, almost courtly man with a fine and delicate sense
of the absurd. Nevertheless, even he has moments in
which he sounds as though he were very seriously
auditioning for a role in an Ionesco play.

On my first morning at my present agency, having
been away from advertising long enough to forget its
precise ambience, I walked down the hall to my new
office to hear outraged bellows emanating from the
art director's office at the end of the hall. "That," my
boss was roaring, "is without a doubt the ugliest egg
suit I have ever seen."

After explaining the situation to me—the agency
was planning to shoot a television commercial star-
ring Humpty Dumpty, and the New York costume

designer who created the egg suit had sent us a sketch
of a demented, leering, mad egg which would have
frightened every child in five states—my boss asked
me what the hell was so funny. I could only gasp
weakly, "Grown men and women, grown-up adult
people . . ." But such is the nature of advertising that
the next such overheard outburst—"Not only did we
lose the dollar-shaped cake pan, we forgot to pay the
midget"—struck me not as absurd but as a genuine,
regrettable agency flub-up. This one does not even
bear explanation. The point is, absurdity is no longer
absurd when it is what you do for money. Otherwise,
I suppose, we would all take to sitting in trees naked,
like Yossarian in *Catch-22*.

There are the real working weirdos, of course. The
most rococo of them, however, work in New York
and make really nauseatingly large salaries at age
twenty-two, and some are downright dangerous-
weird. In 1970, Jerry Della Femina, himself a super-
talented veteran of the New York creative scene,
wrote one of the funniest books I have ever read
about advertising called *From Those Wonderful Folks
Who Gave You Pearl Harbor*, in which he precisely
and beautifully illuminated the psyches of the creative
crazies, and I recommend it for anyone who wants to
meet the guys they're talking about when they say,
"All people in advertising are crazy." These guys really are, from the guy who tried to throw his chair out
the forty-first-floor window onto Forty-third Street to
the art director who stabbed his telephone with a pair
of shears, saying matter-of-factly, "That should hold
it." What comes clear in Della Femina's book is that
the weirdo who is also good and produces lives to
become a real legend, and the weirdos who have

nothing going for them but weirdness don't make it. Which seems only fair to me, but I still don't know another business that will let a guy who eats peanut butter with his feet even have a crack at a job.

I think the days of the great baroque weirdos are probably over now, having died from the same excess of fat that nearly slew the economy in '69–'70. The FCC and HUD cracked down on a lot of the extravagance, too, so the field isn't nearly so attractive to the *rarae aves* who once made so much money and ruckus in it. In a way, it's a shame. What fun they were to watch, and how we envied them here in Atlanta. Money and mores simply have never permitted out-and-out eccentricity for its own sake in the South. Not in business.

What we do have are talented people who are perhaps a little strange in one or two areas, but not all. One of my favorite advertising men in all the world kept a tarantula named Hugo in a cage on his desk; it was a Father's Day present from his boys, and he'd probably still have it except that a new employee saw it and had hysterics, and he was forced to take it to the garage and put it in the trunk of his car, where it contracted grippe and later died. Another friend, a copywriter, ghosts gently around his world oblivious of clothing and shelter; if someone asks him to lunch in a semi-respectable place, it is usually necessary to make him some cuff links for his French cuffs out of paper clips, and when he needs shoes, his wife will call a colleague and ask him to take George out and buy him a pair of shoes and she'll send a check. Another, an account executive, loathes motels and says by way of explanation, "They wrap the soap. They don't wrap the soap in the great hotels of Europe."

One friend kept an ancient and operable wheel-chair in his office and routinely patrolled the halls in it, wearing duck feet he had made out of sheets from a yellow legal pad—or did until he rounded a corner, careening and duck-footed, and ran headlong into a group of new business prospects being ferried through the agency by a frozen-faced account man.

A shy, gentle art director friend draws the most exquisite and beautifully wrought pornography I ever saw into shots of beaches and sunsets and mountains, and once spent three days making a magnificent pop-up penis for a female media assistant to wear to a Halloween costume party.

When a girl with a truly incredible body moved into the apartment complex which is visible out my window and took to sunbathing by the pool every day at eleven, every man in the agency purchased field glasses or telescopes and, upon the shout "Bandit at eleven o'clock," would come stampeding into my office, leaving clients hanging on telephones and meetings unattended. One got a severe nosebleed on my plate-glass window one day, and another stepped on my instep and put me into an Ace bandage for more than a week. I know a senior vice-president at another agency who takes his magazine into the men's room every day at one-thirty and comes out at two. If he's needed, they send for him in there.

These things no longer seem strange to me, if they ever did. I truly can't remember a time when some-body I knew in advertising wasn't engaged in some-thing that might, in a large insurance agency, be deemed a little odd. The thing about all those people I just mentioned is that all are also talented, disci-plined, productive people who get their work done and stay late to meet deadlines. I don't know of any office Christmas parties that turn into orgies; martinis at lunch put almost everybody I know to sleep and so we don't; agency expense vouchers are so elegantly obscure that I fail to see how anyone could successfully pad them; and there are fewer flamboyant affairs in this business than most others I know of. Most of us are too tired, too broke, and don't have time.

The ones I do know of seem to me ill-fated from the beginning. I can't imagine any paramour in her right mind sympathizing with a guy who's down because he couldn't find a white duck for a television spot in St. Petersburg and they had to use a mallard.

The Time of the Party

Sometime around age thirty-five, you think you've finally got it licked. Gold-bitten November is not going to send your sensors pinging this year. The vermeil, Janus-faced specter of Party Time is not going to trick you into something spinning and spangled and foolish *this* season. This year, you're going to grow up.

But it gets you. Or it does me, it always does. Party is the word that unlocks frozen mahogany intentions. Party is the word that has waylaid three centuries of persimmony sanctity. Party is the other side of the pewter coin of Duty, the vulgar ruby in the navel of Seemliness. Maybe at other seasons our hymn-clotted Puritan ancestry goes with us to our fetes and dares us over our shoulders to have a good time. But not in November. This is the time when our older, Spain-spangled blood takes over. November is Party Time.

It's an old sorcery, this party thing that shakes you like a radiant demon terrier. You'll have met it first

when you were about six, and the hour before your
birthday party was an aspic of pure bright terror. The
kids who would—or would not—come to your party
were no longer your dingy-kneed, photo-faced peers.
Surely, when they came through your screen door
with the Big Little Books and the Black Beauty jigsaw
puzzles, they would suffer a party change into something rich and strange. They would be, at that
moment, miniature Merlins with the power to award
you a fleeting, first-grade immortality.

Their not coming was an enormity of disgrace and
betrayal not to be borne.

They came, of course. And did the things that kids
always seem to do at parties, that they never do any
other time. The ethos of a party *is* different. People
don't act the same. Party behavior is a ritual, iron in
its natural laws, but it is a ritual followed only then.
In my childhood, Buddy Carmichael threw up at
every party until he was twelve. Wesley Blalock had a
BB lodged under his eyelid and charged a penny a
feel. Virginia Pringle drew ambitious and lascivious
naked ladies, their hair always the improbable
carmine of well-licked red pencil, on sheets of Blue
Horse tablet paper, also for a penny. I wrote poems
to order, personalized with one's name, for a nickel if
they rhymed or a penny if they didn't, quite. Kids are
not without party talents and do pretty well by them
financially, until puberty and dawning adult inhibi-
tions put the lid on the profitable performing arts.

After twelve, parties changed, though the wonder
remained.

Some of us went away to various schools and
academies and some of us stayed on at the local high
school, but we all learned the immutable litany of the

party ethic. We learned the proper, flat-sweet things to say to the darkling ranks of chaperones. We learned the precise length of time we could sit in our dates' fathers' Chevies behind the gym at intermission without arousing adult suspicion. We learned to dance, whatever prancing thing was popular that year. The sleek, sinuous "good dancer" and the "dresser" had their moments of glory, while the bruised and scabbed Saturday Heroes shuffled like bewildered Clydesdales among ranks of Lipizzaners. We learned the elation of a full dance card or the misery of an empty one; where to wear a corsage (orchids ten points, sweetheart roses, one); how to get white bunny fur off aging tuxedo jackets; what to say about our dates in restrooms that was properly cool without being slanderous when it got, inevitably, back to them.

We learned to drink terrible, cloying stuff in Dixie cups or dumped into ginger-ale-and-lime-sherbet punch, but drinking was never all that much a part of those parties. A party has a quicksilver life of its own, far beyond booze.

A party still has power for me. It still quickens and blooms in that magical, suspended time just before it begins. It will never be realer than it is at that hour, even if it lasts until dawn.

Unfortunately, many of ours do. We don't give many large parties, space and the exchequer being what they are in our house. I'd rather have six or eight people at a time for dinner. Even on this small scale, however, there are more than a few evenings where at least one other couple and I watch the cold, white dawn come seeping in over the overflowing ashtrays and littered album covers. I get more and

more vibrantly alive as the early morning blooms and
am given to urging, "Oh, you don't have to go home
yet; it's early. Let's put on *The Messiah*. Let's put on
Dylan Thomas reading *A Child's Christmas in
Wales*." And we do that, or, if certain of our journal-
istic-type friends are over, we sit up and quote poetry
at each other, or read from my battered old college
anthology of modern verse. The sonorous profundi-
ties floating around my living room at some 4 A.M.'s
are astounding—doubly so in light of the fact that no
one is listening to anyone else. We are, instead, waiting for our own turns.

Most of our friends have long since learned to
ignore my entreaties and go politely home when
they're sleepy, but a few are always good for the long
haul, and they and I and fat Crossroads, who adores
parties, will end up blearily eating scrambled eggs in
my kitchen and not liking each other very much and
wishing we'd gone to bed. I have a childish reluc-
tance to let a good evening slip away and will wear
one out doggedly rather than let it die gracefully and
mercifully by itself. Heyward, who goes sweetly and
abruptly to bed at midnight, no matter who is still
there, has come to loathe Handel and Dylan Thomas
and William Butler Yeats equally and passionately. I
doubt if our next-door neighbors care much more for
them.

The large parties we do give are almost invariably
marathons. Indeed, most of the ones we go to are.
Not all—some are exquisite, structured affairs where
the buffet looks like a full-color Cunard ad and the
guests behave like figures in a Swiss clock. They
come smiling and bobbing in at six and go smiling
and bobbing out at eight-thirty. At these affairs, the

hostess will smile brilliantly at any late-lingerers and say, "Would anyone like a little nightcap?" and her guests obediently refuse the nightcap and go wafting out into the twilight. If I said that at one of my parties, everyone would love a nightcap, and we'd be off to the races. We don't usually know the hosts at these impeccable affairs very well.

The people whose parties we attend—and who come to ours—run largely to advertising, newspaper, television, writer, and artist types. They don't, as types, tend to go home early. They do, as types, tend to drink a lot of booze. This combination makes for interesting parties.

Still, they are predictable parties, in that, when you know the attendees well enough, you know precisely at what time in the evening and at what level on the martini shaker who is going to do what. Our columnist friend is going to mis-recite, "Milton, thou shouldst be living at this hour." Our clever, unhappy copywriter friend is going to make up a slanderous, wildly funny song about someone present and sing it, accompanying himself on his guitar, and the offendee is going to go home in a snit. The Carlyles—the nearest couple we know to Beautiful People—are going to have a white-lipped, hissing fight and she will drive his Mercedes home and he will go to bed in our guest room, where we will find him in the morning in a tangle of slept-in clothes and happy cats.

Heyward will drag out his cache of Glenn Miller records and we will all jitterbug for a while. Margaret, who is hip-deep in Junior League volunteer work, will corner our resident psychiatrist and explain tearfully how she is Wasting Her Life and always wanted to be a nurse. I will corner him and explain that I am

Wasting My Life and always wanted to be a social worker. Our sweet, solemn shrink will remember quiveringly that once he had a chance to play professional baseball. . . .

I guess what saves our parties from what we all sneeringly call Suburban Saturday Soirées is that no one ever seems to go out in the kitchen and neck. Mate-swapping doesn't have a chance with all those taut, flashing egos waiting to be aired. We are all too old and, though we will not own to it, far too conservative for pot. Largely, we are talkers. Oh, great, great talkers.

To outsiders, our parties must have a certain air of Fall-of-Rome depravity. One evening, when we had about fifty people talking and waving stemware and shining their behinds, as my grandmother was wont to describe preening, a truly epic rainstorm began. One of our guests, sensibly departing at a reasonably decent hour, backed two wheels of his shining new Lincoln Continental off the bridge over our creek—a thing that happens with embarrassing regularity even on balmy, bright noons. All attempts to lift or push the car back onto the driveway failed. Rain was sheeting down in horizontal gusts and webs. After calling seven or eight all-night wrecker services, we found one that grudgingly agreed to come over.

Concurrently with this episode, my husband had been amusing a small knot of guests in the kitchen with a description of my new wig. It was long, lush, wildly tousled, streaked blond, magnificent, and a terrible mistake. It did not make me look splendidly leonine like Melina Mercouri. It made me look like I should be hanging around the men's room at the bus station downtown. Heyward thought it would be exceedingly droll to model it, and he put it on, whereupon *he* looked like he should be hanging around the men's room at the bus station. Over his Chevy Chase Club blazer and Colonial Club tie, it was indescribably grotesque. I have seen the same effect in a certain silky gay cabaret on a side street in Old San Juan.

The brouhaha with the crippled Lincoln began then, and in the melee Heyward forgot to remove the wig. The doorbell rang. Heyward opened the door. A soaked teenager in a white garage coverall, with a near crew cut and pearl-downed apple cheeks, stood rooted on the doorstep, white rings around his mouth and eyes. "Somebody called about a car in a creek," he managed to croak, staring like a Medusa victim at my husband. "Oh, yes," said Heyward, oblivious to the impression he was making. "I'll show you." And he did. "Have to get some help," mumbled the stricken boy, and he vrooomed away in his truck and, of course, did not come back. Another guest who had, for some reason, a logging chain in his trunk finally extricated the car.

On the main, our parties are amiable enough; no friendships or marriages have been permanently sundered that I know of, and there is far more vermouth than vitriol at them. I have been to some creative-y parties, however, where abiding hurt and damage were wrought, and they make me look with less than joy on my fellows. One I will always remember for the sheer poetry of the pain inflicted was a large buffet for one of the South's native sons, an internationally acclaimed artist, a real Giant of a Man as it were. The Giant is a frequent guest at conferences and seminars and such around the South and is much admired and sought-after for his rugged eccentricity, his Hemingwayesque aura, his really dizzying talent, and his agate-green eyes. Women cluster around him like yellow jackets around a rotting watermelon rind.

On this particular evening, he was the center of a group of lesser souls, including me, who were listening raptly to his drawling litany of ennui with celebrityhood. Into the circle came a small, pretty woman about forty-five, gloved, hatted, and so obviously somebody's wife and mother back in Lumpkin that you had to smile at her, not in contempt, but in joy and content at the sheer *rightness* of her. "I just had to introduce myself," she said shyly, and her voice skidded around a little in her throat. "You won't remember me, but you gave my watercolor *such* a good criticism at the seminar in Brunswick last fall. I've been to every lecture you've given, and I drove up tonight from home just to meet you." She couldn't stop talking, and we all stared a little hypnotically. "I hoped I could really get to know you. . . ." And her voice fell like a cracked chime at his feet.

"I'm at the Sheraton," said the Giant. "I'm sure you're not going to drive all that way home tonight." And he took out his room key and handed it to her.

She took it. I am sure she was bleeding to death inside, but she took it. I hope his next opening bombs.

Mainly because my own parties are so happily, messily unnoteworthy, I am fascinated with the polished and shining Events described in *Vogue* and *Town & Country*, and have always been sure there was some kind of Rosetta Stone for parties that would help me give mine a touch of class. Oh, not like those in the slicks—I have no pool, no gazebo, and it is unlikely I will ever even lay eyes on Berry

Berenson or Bianca Jagger. But something with a bit more wit, rhythm, and panache. And indeed, there is help at hand, in the pages of those selfsame publications that chronicle the galas of others.

There is in every slick that ever comes off the press a department which will tell you how to have the most marvelous, memorable, elegant, amusing, and erudite party in Christendom—all without working up a sweat. Here, to me, is instant adulation, thunderous acclaim, an immortal reputation as a hostess, the reins of the Good Life. All mine, if I follow the simple, foolproof steps set out to aid me. Do I bite? Of course. With great relish and the world's shortest memory of what happened at my last party, I bite every time. Always more than I can chew.

I can only conclude that the editors who conceive and diagram those *tours de force* either (a) read them in another slick and cribbed them without a trial run, (b) have whole battalions of insanely devoted family retainers, plus a live-in social director, at their command, or (c) don't know the same kind of people I do.

From years of studying failproof party strategy, I have culled a basic list of Ironclad Guarantees, a Five-Foot Shelf for the hostess. And I have learned, soul-deep, what happens when I apply them.

Get help. First and foremost, say the experts, have all or part of your party catered if it's a large one. For years, when I was single, my roommates and I managed teeming throngs of people in a three-room apartment by buying the basic minimum of horrendously bad liquor, pouring it into empty Christmas decanters, setting out peanuts and potato chips, and smiling bravely when the booze ran out. Some

half-waffled guest would invariably offer to run up to
the liquor store and replenish the stock. Those days
pass with maidenhood, however, and you cannot get
by with that sort of chicanery under your own roof.
Comes the day when you want to give a large,
smooth, elegant party. In my case, the first of those
was a no-holds-barred pre-wedding party for dear
friends. Along with two other couples, we planned
lists, sent invitations, ordered flowers, bought a bale
of Pucci between us, borrowed and shined enough
silver to frighten Lloyd's of London, decked my halls
with greenery, damask, tapers. We also cajoled one of
the co-hostesses into pressuring her family's devoted
family retainer to come and buttle. And I blithely
called the Atlanta Press Club and engaged the services of a bartender, who would bring with him, as
per agreement, the liquor, the glasses, the setups, and
the garnishes. In short, we Got Help.

On the night of the party, the house shone like a
Christmas tree, the rented banquet table shivered
under watercressed and shaved-ice-bedded extrava-
ganzas, the Pucci-ed hostesses were fluttering and
glowing, the hosts were expansive, the white-coated
retainer was sullen but at parade rest, the candles
flickered, and the flowers flowered. The bride-and-
groom-to-be arrived. The mother and father of the
bride arrived. Five, ten, fifteen guests arrived. The
bartender, the booze, the setups, the ice, the olives,
lemons, etc., did not.

Finally, a pink-and-gray 1956 Chevrolet careened
up the driveway and the bartender alit—an incredible plastic blonde in black stretch pants, black
sweater, and black, thigh-length vinyl boots. She
looked like she'd just been shipped from Japan and

inflated. "I'm here," she caroled. "Where's the ice and the booze?"

Three hosts went one way for liquor, the father of the bride went another for ice, the groom ran out to rent glasses, and most of the male guests went into the kitchen, where we'd set up the bar, to sample the plastic lady's incomparable expertise in whipping up neat Cokes. The Retainer was quivering with outrage, and I was damning the press club in a manner to discredit all the Pucci in the world. Having been in and around press clubs for some years, I should have known better.

It was a fine night eventually, even though the barmaid left at nine-thirty with a male guest and someone let Peter and the Major, manic with the occasion, out of the basement to run joyfully through the steak tartare. But it was not, I suspect, the sort of affair *Vogue* had in mind.

Mix your guests. The secret of a really stimulating party, say the oracles, is to have on hand a varied and refreshing blend of guests. Aside from the fact that we don't know the sort of variegated people you can assemble like a nosegay, this is out-and-out sudden death to every party I have tested it on. In theory, all those vital, attractive, *different* people will interact chemically on each other, and everyone will learn something fascinating, and the great American god, Good Conversation, will be served. In actuality, however, at my house the lion will not lie down with the lamb, nor the stockbroker with the HEW director, nor the Kennedyphile with the Rockefellerite, nor— adamantly so—the hawk with the dove, no matter how long that's been over. My guests can't even seem to agree on Watergate. These chaotic times are not conducive to graceful, amiable party mixes; indeed, I do well at my parties to keep writers from dismembering other writers. The most radical mix I hope to achieve at future parties is men and women. That's still chic in the South.

Plan your party around a motif. It may be that perfectly charming parties have been hung around a motif. A St. Swithin's Day party in the arbor of a great old estate in Newport might conceivably be enchanting. But to throw a Kentucky Derby Day party in a large "singles" apartment is to cry havoc. I gave one once, on a heady, balmy May day, with mint juleps in frosted silver goblets and Virginia ham and biscuits, for a few selected guests. I even muddled my own mint and made my own simple syrup. One hundred and three people and a sheep dog came, a guy from down the street made a killing taking bets, and someone I'd never seen before came to the party on a motorcycle and won eighty-five dollars.

Serve one special drink. We did once, in the interest of economy and simplicity, serve a tongue-withering concoction called Light Cavalry Punch to a group of twenty on New Year's Eve, when we lived in our first married apartment. I got the recipe from a friend who swore he got it from his Tante Paulette, a maiden lady of great gentility, who lived in New Orleans and grew hydrangeas. It came very close to severing several relationships, including a couple of marriages, and succeeded in summoning four of Atlanta's Finest to the door in response to the Mormon Tabernacle Choir's rendition of "The Battle Hymn of the Republic" at fifty decibels on the stereo.

There are several other party clinchers advocated in the slicks that have aborted in my hands, among them Word Games (my guests will only play dirty-word Probe) and alfresco affairs (somebody brought a keg of coma-inducing homemade wine to the last one of those). I think, however, that from now on I will abide with the peculiar party alchemy that seems to ferment naturally in our house. Legion is its name, and November is its season.

There Was an Old Woman

∞

We met Miz Rosa Sharn Turnipseed on a late November Sunday last year, in the mountains of north Georgia. We usually drive up sometime during the warm autumn to see what fall has done to the mountains. It is a pleasant day's round-trip drive, to touch the flaming ridgepole of the state and brush the North Carolina line and come home again. Georgia's Blue Ridge Mountains are the coccyx of the Appalachians: old, old mountains, born eons ago under a strange, terrible young sun and gentled to softened woman-curves by millions of years of inferno heat and glacier cold and the storms that come screaming over their shoulders every winter. Though I am an ocean creature in my soul, there is to me no hill country on earth quite so splendid as these spasmed old Georgia mountains that mark the dying of the Appalachian chain.

Though they are furred with edge-blurring forests and rounded like supine titans' torsos, they are high mountains. Brasstown Bald, the state's highest peak, soars 4,784 feet into the peculiar blue haze that gives them their name. It is queer air up there. Close, you can see details with the startling clarity that all mountain air seems to have. I have seen quite distinctly the striated bristling of the fur on a small black bear cub, snapped swaying to a pin oak across a valley on a neighboring mountainside. At a distance, you can still see clearly the frozen surf of the mountains washing away into North Carolina, out of sight. The thin scrim of blue that hangs over the hills doesn't obscure, but it colors. Farther north, into North Carolina, where they grow wild and fierce, stretching toward the two-mile-high mark, these mountains are called the Great Smokies, because of that shawling gauze.

It is wild country despite its calm. Even the little towns that are stuck on its wrinkled hide, mostly where one narrow, pitted blacktop state road crosses another or along a skinny, weed-spiked railroad track, seem lean and perfunctory and honed to a razor-backed dangerousness. Mountain towns don't drowse in a thick layer of heat and forgottenness like the little towns of the Georgia plateaus and coastal plain. They bristle like the cockleburs they are, and most of the people in them have a corresponding bare sharpness of shank and face.

Out of the towns and off the main roads, at the end of red clay tracks leading into long valleys and under the frowning foreheads of mountainsides, there are leaning, wide-spaced cabins where the loners, the hill men, live. They farm a little where they can; they hunt, fish, make 'shine, and run it; they feed on aloneness as the city dweller feeds on the anonymous sweat of his shoulder-rubbing fellows. It is a well-known axiom to a Georgia native that one doesn't go into the real hills and mess with the people there. "They'd as soon kill you as look at you" is a gross and unfair exaggeration, but it has one foot in fact as well as one in legend. Proud people, still of face and quick of brushfire temper and largely defeated by the rocky meagerness of their land and lives, they are still not bowed, and do not suffer the cheeky, chatty intrusion of flatlanders and city people with a lot of grace. Many of them are descendants of the original Scottish and English settlers who came to the Appalachians in haste and exile after the battle of Culloden; it is a cherished Georgia belief that there is Stuart blood in those mountains, and it may be so. There are, in fact, somewhere lost up there, dulcimers made by hand, songs that have never been recorded, whole families whose identical faces were cast in the wild west islands of Scotland in another time. They have married each other and fought each other and worked beside each other for hundreds of years, and it is probably long proximity rather than inbreeding that links their sharp shoulders so closely together against the soft, insinuating outsiders.

After James Dickey wrote his stunning *Deliverance*, there was a great outcry against his portrayal of mountain people as brutalized, wounding men capable of murder and homosexual rape. "We are not like that; we are decent, hard-working people, we are our own men," said the letters that came pouring into the city newspapers. And, indeed, they are. But those letters came out of the towns, where tourism and chicken farming and television have painted a gloss of affluence and articulateness over everything. Out of the towns, those are savage hills and rivers, and I do not find it unimaginable that a *Deliverance* might happen on the shouting wastes of the Chattooga, where Dickey set his novel. It is an incident as much of that land as the witless muggings and knifings are of Atlanta's night jungle.

When you have business with the people of the mountains, it is best to conduct it with the same flat, tough, spare courtesy you will be extended. Patronization is a grave error. City-spawned exclamations at the quaintness of mountain crafts and the "characters" who live in the hills are serious breaches of etiquette and sense.

On that Sunday last November, we drove through the little towns linked by the ribbon of the state highway, north through flat country that doesn't rise gradually into mountainhood but jumps abruptly and flatfootedly at the blue bulk of the hills up around Cleveland. The wildfire color of the mountain hardwoods that is so glorious in early October had long since bled away; we were left with the tawny shawls of kudzu and the black skeletons of hardwoods, with the black-green of the evergreens like an animal's undercoat. It was a warm day; Indian summer can come as late as early December to Georgia and might cling tenuously in the sixties for a couple of weeks. It was sunny, but with the pale-lemon sunlight of a southern autumn. We had friends with us, and planned to drive up to Helen, a little mountain town that has recently discovered tourism and quaintness at the same time and has got itself up with ersatz chalet façades and geraniums in window boxes and half-timbered shops extolling souvenirs with hanging signs lettered in curly Bavarian script. In the cool summers, about half the citizenry dons lederhosen

and mans the shops and cafés and makes a killing off
the tourists. It isn't badly done, only strange and
baroque in those bony mountains, and there is at
least one good restaurant open until Christmas, so we
had decided to have lunch there, prowl around a little, and drive back home.

North Georgia has place names like music; I never
tire of them. Warwoman Creek. The towns of Free
Home, Ball Ground, Bannockburn, Flowery Branch,
Social Circle, Rising Fawn, Tiger, Fry. It was near
Suches and Neels Gap, in the vast Chattahoochee
National Forest, that I suddenly remembered a public
campground where we'd stopped a few summers back
to eat a picnic lunch, on the way to spend a weekend
with friends who had a place on Lake Hiawassee. It
had been a dreadful, flat, treeless place then, on a valley plain, full of trailers and campers huddled as close
together as they could get against the ringing blue of
the mountains. There had been perhaps a hundred
people lined up along the lip of a decimated trout
stream: children shrieking in diapers; hot, exasperated
women lining up with other children to use the public
toilet. Flies and plastic wrap swarmed all over the
place, and people sat in folding aluminum chairs outside their camper doors, lifting up their eyes unto the
hills over the heads of their neighbors perhaps five
feet away. I had hated it and don't know why I wanted
to visit it again when I saw its sign beckoning at the
turnoff of the short gravel road that led to it.

But I did, and we drove down the autumn-rutted
road and into the campground.

It was a flat, deserted plain now, like something
that has been hastily tidied up after a war, with only
the concrete dolmens of the trailer hitches rising

stubblelike out of the bare, scuffed earth, and so we saw her immediately. A shapeless, gnome-like pile of an old woman in a bizarre, gypsy-like getup: fringed, multicolored shawl over a black taffeta dress, beaded bag hanging from the hands folded in her lap, high-heeled, pointed-toe, strapped pumps like the ones my mother wore in the twenties that I used to dress up in. And a cloche. An honest-to-God 1920s cloche that jammed down around her ears and disappeared into the hunch of her shoulders. It was made of some sort of stiffened lace or horsehair fabric that I had never seen before.

She was sitting on a cement hitch near the dried-up stream that cuts the camp in half, and she was all alone on that still, lemon plain.

"Well, Jesus," said our friend Sam. Nobody else said anything. In all that ringing quiet, we felt almost frightened of her, armored away though we were inside the carapace of the big Buick. She looked— inevitable. Grotesque, but not out of place. More like some native elemental who only came out when the people left. We could not ignore her, but I desperately wanted Heyward to turn the car around and leave, and perhaps then she wouldn't exist.

We got out of the car in a flying wedge and walked up to her. She looked at us alertly, not with welcome but with the same bright expectation (of whatever was to come) that a tame animal might regard an obviously well-meaning stranger.

"Ma'am, can we help you?" said Heyward, and his voice was as small and without echoes as the report of a cap pistol.

"Nossir," she said. "I reckon they'll be along terreckly."

We looked around idiotically and instinctively; could she be part of a late-camping family? But no, there was no vehicle, no car or trailer.

"Ma'am," I said, "is there somebody coming for you? Are you waiting for somebody?"

Her face changed suddenly, crumpled; incredibly, she was weeping the dry, rusted, tearless sobbing of the very old.

"They ain't nobody comin' for me," she said, and she plucked at the shawl. It was Spanish or Mexican, frayed, and creased as though it had been packed away for a long time, very clean. We could smell moth balls about her. "They left me here and went on. I been right chere since after breakfast."

Dear God, I thought, has somebody really put this old woman out here and gone off and left her? I was angry with her for muddling up my day. I was appalled. I didn't know what to do with this desiccated old woman in her drying twenties finery, and I wanted achingly not to know about her. We were all strangely embarrassed.

"Ma'am." Dorothy tried now. "Ma'am, who left you here?"

"My daughter. My daughter and her husband. We live in . . . Cincinnati. We wuz going home. We been down to see our folks in Florida. I got to acting up." She flashed us a rictus of defiant glee. "I shore can act up when I haf to. They 'uz tellin' me they 'uz gone put me out didn't I hush, and they done it."

Oh, God. She must have been ninety. So frail. Rouge was hectic on her slack cheeks, as soft and crumpled as old-fashioned silk velvet. Lipstick leaked crazily up the creases on her upper lip toward her nose. She didn't sound like an Ohioan; she sounded as rural South as I have ever heard. Still, they could have moved recently. . . .

"What's your name, ma'am?" I asked helplessly. We could not leave her there.

"Rosa Sharn."

"Sharn? Is that your last name?"

"No." Impatiently. "It's Miz Turnipseed. Rosa Sharn's my name."

It dawned on me, the only native Southerner. Rose of Sharon.

"Rose of Sharon?" She nodded, slyly. She wasn't giving away anything.

"That's a pretty name," said Sam, and she nodded gravely that it was.

"What is your daughter's name, Mrs. Turnipseed?" asked Dorothy clearly and roundly. It was a key bone in this insane November game we were playing.

Her face closed as tightly as a walnut. "Don't know."

And that was all we could get out of her. She would speak no more. Sometimes she watched us under the absurd brittle brim of the cloche; her eyes were like tea-brown agates that you could see into. Mad eyes.

But mostly she watched her hands in her black taffeta lap. Gnarled, spotted sassafras roots. And she hummed tunelessly under her breath, swinging the beaded bag in time to her inner music. Once she held out her foot, the ankle elephantine and misshapen with arthritis, blue worms of veins crawling burstingly over it, as if to admire the pinching cruelty of the delicate shoe. The strap cut deep into her swollen instep, almost disappearing. She wore no stockings, and the sole of the shoe had only a few scratches. We were stalemated, frozen like statues. It was after one o'clock, and a flying cloud covered the sun and breathed of winter.

"Are you hungry, Mrs. Turnipseed?" said Heyward abruptly.

"Yessir," she said, and she smiled suddenly and sunnily. "I shore am."

"Let's go get some lunch."

"Ain't got no money." The sly shutter was back over her face. I thought we'd lost her again.

"We'd like you to be our guest." And he offered his arm. Like a tottering, wild old duchess, she took it, and we started for the car, an outrageous entourage around this demented old gargoyle.

I knew what was in Heyward's mind. We would take her into Helen, and while we ate, one of us would unearth a policeman or sheriff and explain our plight, and they could take her over and set in motion the machinery of the search for the fled daughter. We would be absolved. Warm and fed, perhaps, she would tell someone the name, the address in Cincinnati.

"We'll turn up your daughter in no time," I caroled comfortingly, and once again we almost lost her. She stopped and tugged away from Heyward's hand on her arm.

"Well, we'll think about that later," I amended hastily. "Plenty of time after lunch."

So she came with us, and we put her into the back seat with Dorothy and Sam, and we drove away toward Helen.

On the way, Heyward and I conferred in whispers, and Sam and Dorothy made desperate, baited conversation to her. She said almost nothing; she hummed. Once she said, "Look'er there, if that ain't a bee tree I be hanged," and we looked at a tree like all the others. Cincinnati?

And once, in a toneless burst, she said, "They don't treat me good. They put me out on the porch. Vester, he hit me one time, and they drownt my cat."

We rode the rest of the way in pain and silence.

There was a small lunchroom affair on the outskirts of pretty, ridiculous little Helen; it had a gas pump and a screened door with GRO. MEATS. FEED painted on it and a Coca-Cola sign with TATE'S CAFÉ lettered above the brand name. Two or three pickup trucks and a rusting but operable old Chevy said it was open. Tacitly, we abandoned the lunch at the good little restaurant and stopped and went in.

There were a couple of tables covered in oilcloth, and a long counter behind which a man in an army camouflage shirt was talking to a couple of other men seated at stools. He looked at us narrowly, looked again at the old woman. "We'd like to get something hot to eat," Heyward said to him, "and I'd like to use your phone. Could you tell me the police's number? We found this old woman down at the campground; her daughter and son-in-law went off and left her and I need to—"

"Shoot, that's old Miz Turnipseed, and ain't nobody gone off and left her," said the man, who turned out to be the Tate of Tate's Café. "Vester was down here 'bout ten, said she done gone off agin. Cornelia's fit to be tied. I'd call 'em, but they ain't got no phone. I'll git this boy here to run her on home, though."

"We'll do it," said Heyward. I suppose he, like the rest of us, was curious about this old woman's environment. More than that, we were all oddly and deeply involved with her.

"They'll be much obliged," said Mr. Tate.

We fed her first; she had scrambled eggs and grits in a thick, red-rimmed plate, and a cup of murderously black coffee, which she whitened with milk. She doused the whole plate with ketchup, and when we told her we were going to take her home, she came docilely to the car, and she didn't say another word.

Following Mr. Tate's directions, we doubled back past the campgrounds and turned up a narrow, rutted road almost straight up a mountain flank. You wouldn't have noticed it from the state highway if you hadn't been looking for it. We drove a long, grinding, bumping way up under a canopy of black evergreens, and then there was a clearing hacked out of the undergrowth, and in it a mobile home, anchored to the earth. Its furrowed aluminum was weeping rust, and there was a late-model Impala parked in the small, clawed-out yard, and another rusted old junker up on blocks behind the trailer. The trailer hung there so wildly suspended on the mountain that I wondered how they'd ever gotten it up there in the first place.

"Tap your horn a couple of times," I said to Heyward; you do that in the rural South when you approach a stranger's home, and he did. The door opened and a man appeared on the concrete block that served the trailer as a doorstep. He stood very straight and silently. He was a tall man, cadaverously thin, in tan work clothes.

"We've brought Mrs. Turnipseed back," said Heyward, leaning out of the car. The man nodded. A woman appeared in the doorway behind him; she was fat and any age at all, and even from the car we could tell she had been crying. Sam helped the old woman out of the back seat, and the younger woman ran down the step and went to her, and put her arm around her to lead her inside.

"Mama, what you want to do that for?" she said, and that was all she did say. We hung there awkwardly; should we explain where we found her, give them our names?

"We are obliged to you," said the tall man in a rusty, unused voice, and he turned and followed the younger woman and the old woman inside and shut the door. We turned the car around in the small, steep yard; it took a very long time, and Heyward did it very self-consciously, as though eyes were watching us. But I don't think they were.

It was only after we were out on the state road and bowling toward home that anyone spoke. It was Dorothy, and she said, "Those people never beat that old woman."

"No," said Sam. "You could tell they'd never do that. What a grand old liar, though."

I thought about her, that old woman escaped from her mountain in her camphory finery, living far back in her own head with strange, invented violences that must have been, to her, preferable to the measureless, real eternities of the few days left to her. I thought about her, a last blaze of splendor on the loose before the long dark.

"It isn't so much that she was lying, maybe," I said. "She was sort of like a leaf that turns red and then dies. I mean, a leaf is just as real when it's suddenly turned red and strange as it was when it was green . . . it was her Indian summer."

It was a murky and fervidly romantic analogy, and
it got the silence from the back seat that it deserved.
We were mainly quiet until the gap-toothed grin of
the city skyline came up ahead of us to the south, and
then we went back to our house and watched the end
of the pro game.

Christmas Country

L ast Christmas, for the first time in my life, I didn't spend Christmas at anybody's home—my own, my parents', or Heyward's parents'. We went, instead, to Jamaica, back to the graceful white inn in Ocho Rios where we'd spent our honeymoon.

I had wanted to go back for a long time. I remembered our honeymoon as an enchanted, flawless ten days in a slow, formal, timeless place where brilliant flowers spilled over a concrete balustrade down to a white beach and an incredible, hot, milky blue sea. I remembered elegant black Palmer, the maître d', whose speech was the unforgettable, Oxford-brushed music of the British Caribbean, who had smuggled us an illicit bottle of rum our first night there. I remembered the charming British lady, a friend of friends back in Atlanta, who had had us for drinks on the terrace of her villa on the very lip of a cliff. When I had admired her magnificently ruffed Persian, she'd said, "Oh, Jimmy. Noël gave him to me," and when we'd signed her guest book, we saw by the signature above ours that she did, indeed, mean Noël Coward.

I remembered the sudden thick, black tropical nights and the yellow birds that ate the sugar from the sugar bowl on our balcony at breakfast, and I forgot the crippling sunburn and the idiotic quarrel born of wedding exhaustion, and the sea urchin I stepped on, and I thought Christmas in Jamaica was a fine idea.

But it wasn't. The inn was still indolent and lovely, the warm web of the tropics still jeweled with small sorceries; Palmer was still there, and we called on Duse Hodge and she was still charming, and Jimmy still plumed around our ankles speaking breathy Persian. The sugar birds came back, and we got splendid tans, and sailed and swam and ate a lot of conch chowder and drank a lot of rum. But it wasn't a fine idea.

The inn had the great good sense not to string Christmas lights from the palms or put up a tree, and nobody treated us to Christmas carols from a steel band, and the only nod to the season was a roast beef and Yorkshire pudding on Christmas Day and a Boxing Day picnic at Dunn's River Falls. Tanned, handsome people from the States had a wonderful time, and more than one said how marvelous it was to be there, instead of back in the cold, slushy cities in the middle of the gruesome caricature that Christmas had become. Heyward and I assured everybody and ourselves that it was indeed a marvelous place to spend Christmas.

But it still wasn't a fine idea for us. It was an out-of-kilter, anxious time, as though we had begun a journey and ended up at the wrong place, and they were waiting for us at our real destination. And that was true. It was the wrong country.

It wasn't Christmas country.

It is perhaps a childish and wistful conceit, but the special country of Christmas is vivid and palpable to me. It is a place, a destination. You work through summer, through autumn, through the sorrowing waste of November. And there it is. It has been so, for me, since I was very small, and I think it will always be so.

What you see from the threshold of Christmas is yours alone, your own inner landscape. My Christmas country is forever that of a small southern town in the soft, wet, gray days of December, when street lights wear opal collars. The time is always first dusk, when the lopsided evergreen trees in front of the freight depot bloom into primary colors, the wounded gaps where the power lines go through obscured in radiant clouds of Christmas light. Stores stay open late. The drugstore smells of Evening in Paris gift sets and cardboard-stale chocolate-covered cherries, and the dime store is glorious with tin gadgets and accordion-folded red paper bells, which will blossom out like Christmas roses.

White frame houses have pyramid-shaped electric candles in their windows, in front of the Venetian blinds, and their doors are dressed in foil, pine boughs, flat candy canes of red and white oilcloth. They are in full-dress regalia for the Garden Club decorating contest. One affluent door, more sophisticated than its fellows, wears a paper Santa Claus bought in Atlanta, and it never wins the prize.

Inside, in living rooms warm from coal fires in iron grates, Christmas trees are mostly pine, cut from somebody's woods or calf pasture and brought home behind a Ford tractor. The lights on them don't wink or bubble or twinkle. They go out frequently, with sullen abruptness, darkening one side of the tree and precipitating a scrambling search in the nest of extension cords buried in tissue paper underneath. But they give a sweet and sturdy light, and their heat on the drying needles produces a wonderful smell. That smell, and the exotic musk of cold oranges in Christmas morning stockings, is the official smell of Christmas to me still.

There is a manger scene on the brown lawn of the Methodist church, with a manger of rough-sawn planks made by the Men's League, a heavy cardboard Joseph and Mary, real straw, and an electric light bulb secreted in the straw to indicate the luminous presence of the Child. It is put up three weeks ahead of Christmas, our town's official announcement that the Day will come again this year.

Farther on in Christmas country, there will be the traditional Methodist church Christmas tree, and a giant cedar will be donated and decorated and propped in secular glory at the red velvet altar cushion. Everyone will draw names and on the night of the Tree, the sanctuary will peal with oohs and ahs and you-*shouldn't*-haves, and the giddy giggling of children. Everyone gets a gift. When I was very small, about three, my father was superintendent of the Sunday school and made an announcement early in December that the tree festivities would be held on such-and-such a date. I am told I escaped the clutches of my stricken mother, lurched down the aisle to where he stood, shrieked, "Preach some more about the Christmas tree, Daddy," had a truly heroic

tantrum when he tried to quiet me, and was taken out
in howling disgrace. A lot of my parents' friends still
remember it.

About the time of the church Christmas tree, there
will be a pageant, and the young of the church will be
dressed in assorted biblical raiment and drilled and
rehearsed and, finally, driven stiff-legged and
numbed with terror out into the choir loft to reenact
the Nativity. Throughout all the Christmases—for
they roll into one and become, instead of times, mile-
posts in Christmas country—I had some part in the
pageant. Once, an angel, in a sheet, flapping great
bumbling wings made of more sheet stretched over
fencing wire and festooned with silver tinsel. Once,
owing to a dearth of willing young men, a shepherd,
in my father's maroon flannel bathrobe, with a tur-
ban made from a scarf. Once, in my early teens, a
sullen and mortified Mary with a pillow under my
choir robe. The reluctant Joseph to my Mary was a
senior in high school and president of the Methodist
Youth Fellowship, and I had a hopeless, aching, silent
crush on him. I shall never forgive the pageant director, who said loudly just before we made our
entrance, "For goodness' sake, Hal, hold her arm.
And slow it down, Anne. You're *pregnant.*"

On Christmas Eve, there are carols sung on front
lawns courtesy the MYF—galoshed and muffled
against the raw silver fog that always shrouds this
Christmas country—and people with sweaters thrown
around their shoulders stand shivering on front
porches and applaud the bleating "Si-i-i-lent Night!
Ho-o-o-ly Night!" Somehow the night is, for a while,
silent and holy.

Sometimes Coca-Cola is proffered to the carolers,

and rich, heavy fruitcake made the year before in enamel pans and soaked all year with homemade wine under white muslin. On every hearth, another bottle of Coca-Cola and another slab of winy fruitcake waits for Santa Claus—surely a tipsy, reeling Santa when he finishes his rounds in our town. Cake and cola are always polished off by resigned parents.

On Christmas Eve, sleep is an unimaginable agony. I remember tossing mutely for what seemed black eternities, listening for the rattle of the lock at our front door that meant Santa Claus was coming in. I accepted the fact that he had to use the door because our chimneys were too small as unquestioningly as I accepted the profusion of Salvation Army Santas on every Atlanta street corner. I even bought it when I was told that in Fairburn he came in a truck, the climate being unsuitable for delicate reindeer hoofs. I don't remember the why of that. Otis Fletcher told me there was no Santa Claus when we were in the third grade; I must have been nearly eleven when I concluded that Otis hadn't been lying after all.

You do sleep, of course, though you will swear afterward you never closed your eyes. I took a solemn oath one Christmas, to my parents, that I had not only heard Santa Claus come in, but had seen him, and moreover, that Jack Benny and Mary Livingstone were with him. Whether to nip a budding liar in the bud or shatter one of childhood's most precious myths must have been a real dilemma for my parents. They solved it by admitting that perhaps I *had* seen Santa Claus, but I must have dreamed Jack Benny and Mary Livingstone, as they lived in Hollywood, California, and couldn't possibly have made it to

Fairburn, Georgia, and back in time for their own Christmas morning.

You wake at four and creep into your parents' room. "Is it time?"

"No. Go back to bed."

And at five. And at five-thirty. At six, finally: "All right. It's time." Throughout my Christmas country, kids skin into bathrobes and slippers with bunny ears and race for the living room at six o'clock in the morning.

It is radiant and strange in the black pre-dawn. The tree is aflame. There is a coal fire burning. The Coca-Cola and fruitcake are gone; not a crumb remains. There are the presents brought by Santa Claus, piled unwrapped before the tree. The ones from parents and relatives have been wrapped and under the tree for two weeks, shaken into near-oblivion.

Somehow, the presents all seemed to be the same present, though, of course, they varied. From Santa Claus, a doll every year. One year she cried, another year she drank from a bottle and wet, one year she had "magic baby skin," one year she was an eternal bride-to-be, as frozen on the eve of her wedding as Keats's unravished bride of quietness. One year, when I was twelve, she was a truly exquisite Alice in Wonderland, a perfect, fragile mini-woman. Later that day, goaded by God knows what mute rebellion, spoiled perversity, what rampaging new hormones, I shot her with a new Daisy Air Rifle. My mother cried, and I cried, and my father confiscated the air rifle. Dolls were gone from my Christmas country after that, to be replaced by charm bracelets and pink angora sweaters and record albums, by the flimsy, useless, spangled Christmas things that I still love to receive.

There would be outfits. A nurse's outfit. A cowgirl outfit, complete with fringed vest, six-shooter, and miniature Western boots. An appalling WAC outfit, for we seemed perpetually at war in that holiday country. Somewhere in my parents' house, small, grave me sights along the six-shooter into the camera still; lumpy, unlovely me salutes an unknown commander-in-chief under the patent-leather bill of a hideous, flat-topped cap.

For my mother, a huge jar of blindingly purple bath salts that stank for days when she opened it. I had had my eye on it at Vickers's Five-and-Ten for half a year, and Mrs. Vickers had had to scrape the grime of unwantedness out of its mock cut-crystal when I purchased it. My father would open the miniature hatbox with the wonderful, perfect little hat in it, and a certificate that said he could receive the hat of his choice at an Atlanta hattery. Always, he said it was just exactly what he needed. Always, he bought the same hat.

Then Nellie would come from her small house directly behind ours, through the shrubbery hedge, to receive her ritual black rayon dress and help my mother begin our marathon Christmas dinner, and the current white spitz dog, one of an endless procession emanating from my grandfather's farm, would get his wrapped can of horsemeat, and I would be sent to put on the burgundy velvet dress with the handmade white lace collar my grandmother made me every year. Relatives were coming.

Christmas dinner is always at noon in that country, and there are aunts and uncles, cousins who will break your toys by midafternoon, grandparents in unaccustomed ties and socks with clocks on them, and cameo brooches. Not all can come because of gas rationing, but an uncle who has a C card will collect those on his route, and they will arrive about eleven in the morning, bearing more wrapped presents and shouting, "Merry Christmas! Merry Christmas!" Maddened and made insatiable by largesse and lagniappes, the cousins who have been your good and true companions all year, co-authors of endless, creative mischief, will dismiss your doll with a sniff, have a gaudier outfit than yours, give you a frog on your bicep. A warm-up pre-dinner quarrel will be arbitrated, and you will be sent into the guest bedroom to color in the *Gone With the Wind* coloring book and be quiet. You are, for a little while.

Almost certainly there is a piano in some kept-for-company front room, with a bench full of Scotch-taped sheet music and a dead key or two. A cousin known to be musical plays the measured old anthems of Christmas from a *Broadman Hymnal*, and the family gathers around to sing. An uncle booms out "We Three Kings," the living room fire snickers softly behind its screen, and the fragrance of dinner from the kitchen is frankincense and myrrh.

And finally, after the most spectacular wrapping paper is folded away for next year, the handmade papier-mâché ashtrays admired, the cap pistols taken away, the tearful smallest cousin consoled and his tormentors chastised—Christmas dinner. The dining room table, awkwardly resplendent in company damask and awash in warm fragrances from the kitchen, groans under the ritual feast that never varies. Corn bread dressing. Sweet potatoes with raisins in orange cups, capped with marshmallows. Pickled peaches, cranberry sauce, summer's sweet corn, and butter beans from the row of jeweled jars in the cellar. Ambrosia and fruitcake. And, of course, the imperial turkey. No frozen, giant-breasted, butter-basted bird this, but a proper fowl who was alive two days before in a neighbor's barnyard. This is not to be dwelt on, and isn't.

But before the passing around and the clamor for the drumsticks begin, there is the quiet ritual among the tall, flickering Christmas candles of the paying of a debt of gratitude.

Late in the graying afternoon, after naps and mints and a little more coffee and "How about just a little piece of Grace's coconut cake?" a new camera will be brought out, and the Christmas-worn family will be lined up around the already superannuated tree, and another landmark will be inked forever into the map of Christmas country. To become the Christmas the baby was a year old . . . the Christmas Uncle Harvey knocked over the tree . . . the Christmas it snowed . . . the Christmas the children on the McNeil side of the family got German measles . . . the best Christmas, the prettiest tree, the most fun ever.

There are other Christmas countries, as many as there are people for whom there is Christmas. They are better than mine, or worse, or perhaps only very different. They are cities, or they are farms in Nebraska, or they are strip-mining towns in West Virginia, or they really are Jamaica. Or Las Vegas, or somewhere else sun-smitten and stark and wholly unimaginable to me. There are, of course, many Christmas countries that are terrifying, howling, empty places. Christmas is a mocking and bitter time to many people; I have friends who truly hate and fear it, and my own Christmases now are brushed, however fleetingly, with loss, soiled and used up after Christmas Day. But I know what it is that I have lost, and these present Christmases don't belong in that other Christmas country, though these are warm, rich, good holidays and will undoubtedly be another, a different country, to me one day. Those others belong in childhood, the only one I will ever know, and the only one you will, and that is where I want to go each year.

They are made of garishly sentimental cloth, those places where Christmas is. Part synthetic cloth for many of us, wholly fabricated for others. But they are as real as the places we live now. Because some small, crying thing in us goes home again for Christmas every year, however briefly and reluctantly, and so for all of us there is, indeed, a Christmas country.

It is the country of the human heart.

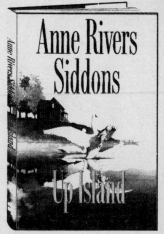

A Tale of Personal Renewal and Transformation
from *New York Times* bestselling author

ANNE RIVERS SIDDONS

Caroline Aubrey Gentry was living the life she was born to—a magnificent home, endless rounds of country club luncheons and cocktail parties, and a comfortable, if passionless, twenty-year marriage to a real estate tycoon.

Then her husband begins his next venture—building a resort on the South Carolina low country island that is the last safe haven for a band of wild ponies. Steeped in low country heritage, the island is also home to fond memories from Caroline's youth. Spurred to action, Caroline must reach deep within herself to save this special place, and to find meaning and purpose in her privileged life.

ISBN 0-06-017616-4
$25.00/$36.50 (Can.)

HarperCollins*Publishers*
www.harpercollins.com

COLONY

In this unforgettable story of love, acceptance, and tradition, Siddons paints a portrait of a woman determined to preserve the spirit of past generations—and the future of a place where she became who she is.
"Outstanding."—*New York Times*

KING'S OAK

Wealthy Andy Calhoun leaves behind a disastrous marriage for the pleasures of small-town life. What she discovers is passion, intensity, and the decision of a lifetime.
"Defies you to put it down."
—*Los Angeles Times Book Review*

HEARTBREAK HOTEL

Born to be well bred, nothing should have disturbed Maggie Deloach's perfect life. But amid the stifling heat of an Alabama summer, something does. And it will change forever how she sees herself and the world.
"An absolute gem."
—*Richmond New Leader*

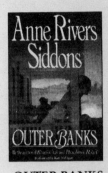